THE NABATAEANS
IN
HISTORICAL
PERSPECTIVE

John Irving Lawlor

BAKER BOOK HOUSE
Grand Rapids, Michigan

To
Mary Ellen, my wife,
and
Karis Lynn and Nancy Lea,
my two daughters.
In appreciation
for their love, encouragement,
and faithfulness.

ISBN: 0-8010-5536-9

Printed in the United States of America

Contents

List of Illustrations

List of Maps

Foreword

Most of us have heard of Petra, "the rose-red city half as old as time," which was literally carved out of the sandstone mountains by a people known as Nabataeans, successors to the Biblical Edomites, the sons of Esau. Some of us will recall that the modern Israelis were inspired by the success of these Nabataeans in developing methods of dry farming and in finding ways of conserving and using such moisture as can be found in the largely barren southland known as the Negev.

It was in 1812 when John Lewis Burckhardt identified Petra and saw its ruins. Prior to that time, the existence of Petra and its significance were completely unknown in the Western world. Even after Burckhardt's discovery, visits to the area were difficult, and few travelers and explorers of the nineteenth century got as far as Petra. The twentieth century has seen not only Petra, but a whole series of Nabataean cities excavated and their remains studied. Professor Lawlor has gathered together a body of knowledge gleaned from literary and archaeological sources to help us understand the Nabataeans in their historical and cultural setting.

The Nabataeans appeared too late in history to be discussed in books on Old Testament archaeology. It was during the second and first centuries b.c. that the Nabataean Arabs, with cultural influences both from the Edomites (later known as Idumaeans) and the Greeks, developed trade routes to carry products from southern Arabia and merchandise from the east—as far away as Africa, India, and China—to "the west," which included both Greece and Italy, along with nearby Syria and Egypt.

Petra was the caravan city through which this merchandise passed. From Petra, a caravan route extended northwestward through Eboda (Abda, Avdat) a major crossroads in the Negev. Here was an important temple and an encampment for Nabataean troops. The caravans with goods for the west went to the port city of Gaza where goods were transferred to ships bound for Greece, Italy, and other lands. To facilitate trade, the Nabataeans built frontier posts with watchtowers and fortresses, financed by duty imposed on the merchandise carried by the caravans. In addition to trade, the Nabataeans were skilled agri-culturalists—building dams and cisterns to make use of the little rain that did fall in the Negev. As a result, the Negev was spotted with settlements, in an area that was sparsely settled before the Nabataean period, and which is today only beginning to assume the character of Nabataean times by the patience and industry of the modern Israelis.

In A.D. 106, Trajan's legate of Syria, A. Cornelius Palma, put an end to Nabataean autonomy and incorporated the Nabataean lands into the Roman Empire. The province thus formed was named *Provincia Arabia*. Life continued under the Romans, and the Byzantine remains of the Negev show a continuity with earlier Nabataean art and culture. The Romans and their Byzantine successors ruled vast areas, of which the Nabataean lands were only a part. New trade routes came to replace those of the Nabataeans. The Moslem conquest proved the death blow to the former Nabataean settlements and culture. The desert encroached upon the remains of Nabataean cities, and their existence was forgotten until our day when archaeologists and Israeli pioneers again go to the Negev.

Charles F. Pfeiffer
Central Michigan University
Mount Pleasant, Michigan

Acknowledgments

The efforts of many individuals have helped make the production of this book possible. The author expresses his sincere appreciation to the following individuals: Mrs. Eleanor K. Vogel, who stimulated the writer's interest on the subject of the Nabataeans and generously financed a trip from Jerusalem to Petra and Aqabah (including several other Nabataean sites en route) in 1967.

Mr. Jay Long, who proofread the manuscript and gave very helpful grammatical suggestions concerning it.

Mr. David McClain, who proofread the manuscript, assisted in research, and prepared the indices.

Dr. George Ernest Wright, President of American Schools of Oriental Research, who granted permission to use many photographs under ASOR's copyright.

John I. Lawlor
Baptist Bible College
Clarks Summit, Pennsylvania

Introduction

Dr. Nelson Glueck, now deceased, stated that the Nabataeans were ". . . one of the most remarkable people that ever crossed the stage of history."[1] That statement was based upon a great deal of research and exploration. Probably no human will ever fully know just how remarkable a people they were. But through the extensive study of many scholars, a great deal of information has been unearthed—both figuratively and literally. Much has been written about them. As a matter of fact, Dr. Glueck devoted one entire volume of some size to a presentation of their history.[2] Little did the Nabataeans realize, when they began their rise to prominence, how greatly they would influence their contemporaries. They knew nothing of the great number of pages that would be devoted to the telling of their history down through the centuries. Yet they themselves "wrote" line after line of inscription in rock, leaving those inscriptions in many different areas of the then-known world. These numerous inscriptions have contributed greatly in piecing together their history. Most assuredly they did not know that one of the most outstanding aspects of their unique culture would be revived some two thousand years later by a different nation liv-

1. Michael Evenari and Dov Koller, "Ancient Masters of the Desert," *Scientific American* 194, no. 4 (April 1956): 40.
2. Nelson Glueck, *Deities and Dolphins* (New York: Farrar, Straus and Giroux, 1965).

ing in much the same territory as they had occupied centuries before.[3]

History seems to lend itself to the interpretation that the Nabataeans were a people of paradox. On the one hand they were a rough, rugged type of people, capable of surviving in the deserts of the Negev and Southern Arabia. On the other hand they were a highly civilized, cultured people, capable of "building" a capital such as Petra and capable of developing a highly organized society. That the latter is especially true is evidenced by the fact that such a comparatively small nation (small in comparison to other nations such as Egypt, Israel, and, of course, Rome) enjoyed such widespread success.

REASONS FOR STUDYING THE NABATAEANS

It is no wonder, then, that the Nabataeans should be a subject of interest to the students of history. The period of their existence (about 700 B.C. to A.D. 100), coupled with their geographic location, would also indicate that a study of their history would be of interest to students of the Bible. Two reasons for such a study have just been indicated. These and other reasons are discussed in more detail on the following pages.

Historical

Not only is the history of the Nabataeans fascinating: it is enlightening as well. Without a doubt their role in the course of history influenced the history of other contemporary nations. Rome, for example, was influenced by the Nabataeans. This is demonstrated by the fact that upon several occasions Rome's efforts, both military and political, were exercised toward them. Josephus and other early historians tell of the constant communication between the two civilizations. Why should Rome have such a great interest in the Nabataeans? Crystal M. Bennett, a present-day authority on the Nabataeans, points out a couple of reasons for such interest:

---

3. I have particular reference here to their water conservation system as it was used in agriculture. The Israelis are experimenting with this, and this shall be dealt with in full detail later.

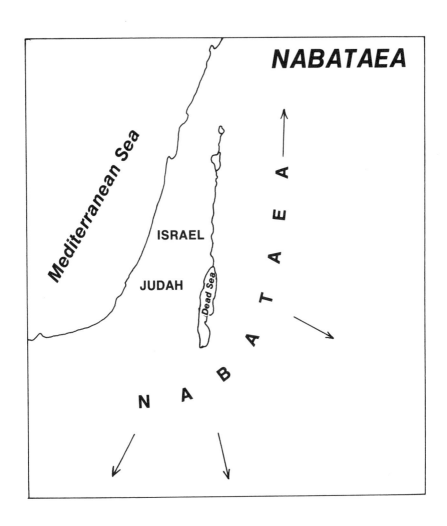

NABATAEA

Mediterranean Sea

ISRAEL

JUDAH

Dead Sea

N A B A T A E A

It was inevitable that the kingdom controlled from Petra should arouse the cupidity of the Roman Empire. Apart from its importance as a buffer state between the nomadic tribes of the Arabian hinterland and the settled coastal regions, its great wealth was a magnet.[4]

The great wealth of the Nabataeans was an attraction not only to Rome but to other people as well. Other areas of Nabataean influence upon the history of contemporary nations, as well as succeeding ones, will come to light throughout this study.

Cultural

Diodorus of Sicily referred to the Nabataeans as "barbarians."[5] Exactly what he meant by this is hard to say, especially in light of the fact that in other places he described them in more favorable terms. It seems impossible to reconcile such a reference with many of the outstanding features of their culture, such as their water-conservation systems, methods of agriculture, architecture, and many other evidences of their well-developed culture. Perhaps it was because they did not speak Greek.

The effects of their culture were widespread. Several contemporary nations felt the impact of the Nabataean culture. A student of Nabataean history has written: "With the small amounts of evidence it probably cannot be proved, but it would seem that the Nabataean caravan routes laid the foundation for Roman politics in the Syrian East."[6] This seems to be a legitimate conclusion. Another writer went so far as to refer to the Romans as "The Nabataeanized Romans."[7] This perhaps is going a little too far, but without a doubt the Romans and others were influenced to a considerable extent. The greatest degree of influence

---

4. Crystal M. Bennett, "The Nabataeans in Petra," *Archaeology* 15, no. 4 (Winter 1962): 233.
5. Diodorus, *Diodorus of Sicily*, trans. C. H. Oldfather, et al., Loeb Classical Library, vol. 10 (New York: G. P. Putnam's Sons, 1933), pp. 103-105.
6. J. M. Riddle, "Political History of the Nabataeans from the Time of Roman Intervention until Loss of Independence in 106 A.D." (M.A. thesis, University of North Carolina, 1961), p. 24.
7. William Libbey and F. E. Hoskins, *The Jordan Valley and Petra* (New York: G. P. Putnam's Sons, 1905), p. 66.

Close-up of the top of the el-Khazneh in Petra. *John I. Lawlor*

was felt by later nations and empires. Glueck makes this point:

> One of the recurrent miracles of history is contained in the fact that . . . the Nabataeans were able at a favorable juncture of events to create a unique civilization, full of achievement and color. When it was overwhelmed in due course of time by forces stronger than it could cope with, it did not just fade away. It transmitted not only its wealth of possessions and accomplishments but also its warmth and creative spirit to those who took over its inheritance. Much of the brilliance of the Byzantine civilization in the Negev may be attributed to the legacy left it by the pagan Nabataeans.[8]

There are many distinct aspects of the Nabataean culture, all of which contribute to the fame of this people of the Inter-Testamental period. Architecture was certainly one such distinctive aspect of their civilization. Speaking of the architecture displayed in

---

8. Nelson Glueck, *Rivers in the Desert* (New York: American Book–Stratford Press, Inc., 1959), p. 242.

the city of Petra, the Nabataean capital, Philip C. Hammond remarks:

> Here is probably the best example of the desert culture that brought Petra to her zenith and made her the queen of a thousand commercial holdings, ruling the trade routes that were avenues of culture from the fourth century B.C. to the end of the first century of the present era.[9]

Other unique features of their culture will be considered at a later point in some detail. This should suffice in pointing out the significance of the Nabataean culture.

Archaeological

Many of these aspects—the historical, the cultural, and the archaeological—blend together and are very closely related. Yet, while this is true, they are distinct aspects in themselves; and each would lend itself to an independent study. From the archaeological standpoint, the Nabataeans have been the object of much study. In the previous century, what little work was done in this area was cursory, and as a result many first thoughts and theories have since been demonstrated to have been erroneous. It is just in the last half century that the bulk of archaeological explorations into their past has been done. But during this comparatively short period of time, great strides have been made in reconstructing their history. Such progress has been greatly assisted by new and improved methods of archaeological study. This is not to say that this field of study has been exhausted. As is true in practically every archaeological period, much work is yet to be done. Therefore, the Nabataean civilization remains a subject of intense interest to all archaeologists and students of archaeology.

Without a doubt, the archaeological approach to their study has made possible the greater share of the cultural information that is available today; and it has assisted in clarifying and confirming much of the historical information. Probably the greatest contributor to the reservoir of archaeological information was Dr. Nelson Glueck, former president of Hebrew Union College

---

9. Philip C. Hammond, "Rose-Red City of Petra," *Natural History* 73, no. 2 (February 1964): 17.

PLAN 4

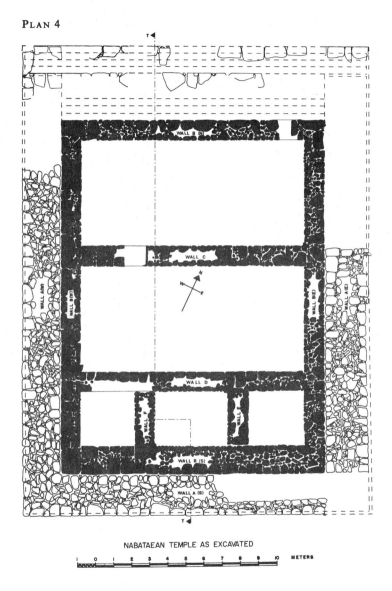

NABATAEAN TEMPLE AS EXCAVATED

Floor plan of the Nabataean temple and walls as excavated at Dhiban by Tushingham. *ASOR (American Schools of Oriental Research)*

Typically decorated Nabataean sherds from Petra. *John I. Lawlor*

and Jewish Institute of Religion in Cincinnati, Ohio. In the early thirties, and again the early fifties, he made archaeological exploratory expeditions into eastern and western Palestine, respectively. As a result of these two extensive exploratory trips, he observed and investigated more than five hundred distinctively Nabataean sites.[10] The identifying feature at each of these sites was the unmistakable Nabataean pottery or pottery remains. This in itself gives evidence of the important role that archaeology has played in the rediscovery of their history. In addition to this one,

---

10. Yaakov Morris, *Masters of the Desert* (New York: G. P. Putnam's Sons, 1961), p. 57.

several other characteristically Nabataean features have been brought to light through the work of the archaeologist.

Biblical

Chronologically, the period of Nabataean prominence was primarily the Inter-Testamental period. For this reason, they were a people related to both the Old and the New Testaments. Though they are never specifically mentioned in either Testament, one of their kings is.[11] The context of this particular Biblical reference indicates that Paul was speaking of his experience in Damascus, which at that time was ruled by a governor who was under a Nabataean king. This, of course, raises some very interesting questions. Some Biblical scholars, historians, and archaeologists are of the opinion that there are a few allusions to them in the Old Testament, though they are not named. In addition to this, there are at least three specific references to them in the Books of Maccabees. Twice they are referred to as the "Nabathites";[12] and once they are referred to as the "Arabians."[13]

Their geographical location put them in direct contact with the nation of Israel. History confirms the continual contact between the two nations. The nature of their relationship fluctuated, however; for at times they were at war with each other, whereas at other times they apparently were allies. Aside from the military and political contacts between the two, there were contacts and relationships of other kinds. Glueck speaks of this:

> When we think of Palestine about two thousand years ago, we often overlook the fact that the Nabataeans were very much a part of its general cultural world. The Judaeans and the Nabataeans knew each other well. There must have been much intermarriage between them. The Judaean king, Herod the Great, for instance, had Nabataean blood. While his father, Antipater, was of Indumaean ancestry, his mother was of Nabataean origin.[14]

---

11. In II Cor. 11:32, Paul speaks of ". . . Aretas, the king. . . ."
12. I Macc. 5:25; 9:35.
13. II Macc. 5:8. There is no question about the identity of the "Arabians" with the Nabataeans in this reference for two reasons: (1) Aretas is named as their king, and (2) Josephus and other historians often refer to them as "the Arabians."
14. Glueck, *Rivers in the Desert,* p. 191.

A similar example of the contact between the Jews and the Nabataeans was the marriage of Herod Antipas, the son of Herod the Great, to the daughter of Aretas IV, one of the most powerful and competent Nabataean kings. While it lasted, this marriage helped to bolster the relationship between them. Later, however, Herod Antipas divorced the daughter of Aretas to marry his own niece and sister-in-law, Herodius. This ruptured any good relationship between the two rulers. Josephus simply says, ". . . Aretas made this the first occasion of his enmity between him and Herod, who had also some quarrel with him about their limits at the country of Gamalitis."[15] One of the results of this series of events was that John the Baptist was beheaded. He had condemned Herod for marrying Herodias, so Herod put him in prison. This, subsequently, led to his martyrdom.[16]

The years of contact between Israel and the Nabataeans, together with the frequent interference of Rome, produced an abundance of intrigue. All the events that took place in the land of Palestine during the Inter-Testamental period, as well as all the people involved in these events, formed the background for the New Testament period—and thus were instrumental in shaping it.

SOURCES OF STUDY

Unfortunately, the Nabataeans had no one who systematically recorded their deeds so that such might be preserved for succeeding civilizations. Therefore, we must rely on such classical works as Josephus, Strabo, Plutarch, Pliny, and others for the bulk of our information. In more recent years, the science of archaeology has greatly assisted in reconstructing the story of their civilization and culture. Through the uncovering of coins, inscriptions, and other archaeological remains, much has been learned about them. These, then, are the two main sources of information about their past: literary and archaeological. Either without the other would be insufficient.

---

15. Flavius Josephus, *Antiquities of the Jews* in William Whiston, trans., *The Life and Works of Flavius Josephus* (1867; reprint ed., Grand Rapids: Kregel Publications, 1964) XVIII. 5.1.
16. Matthew 14:1-12.

Literary

Probably the most voluminous of literary sources are the Flavius Josephus works—*Wars of the Jews* and *Antiquities of the Jews.* Not only are his works voluminous, but they are the best in the sense of accuracy. No historian's works are free from interpretation, however; and this is where the reader must exercise caution when dealing with Josephus. One writer has said:

> . . . he was not only pro-Roman, but also an apologist for the Jewish people. As an historian Josephus seems quite fair but, when it comes to drawing interpretations, he functioned as a propagandist. . . . A rule of thumb in reading Josephus is to remember that whenever he found it possible, he exalted the Maccabees and degraded the Zealots.[17]

This means that when the Nabataeans came in contact with these various factions, such events were interpreted in light of such prejudices.

Rapp says that Josephus is trustworthy for the period of 175 B.C. and later, but earlier than that ". . . it is a completely different situation. . . ."[18] If this be true, and in all probability it is, Josephus's handling of Nabataean history should be largely accurate; for he does not deal with them to any extent prior to that period. The main problem that might arise is his interpretation of some aspects of that history.

Another major literary source is Strabo's *Geography.* It is apparent that he was somewhat knowledgeable about Arabia, the Mediterranean Sea, the Red Sea, and the Dead Sea. But where did he get his information? Falconer informs us that the majority of his information came from two individuals: Agatharchides and Aelius Gallus.[19] The latter was a friend of Strabo. About 25 B.C., Gallus, at the order of Augustus, led an expedition through Arabia. For his guide, he had the Nabataean Syllaeus. The expedition was a complete failure; and Gallus blamed Syllaeus, his

17. Riddle, "Political History of the Nabataeans," p. 24.

18. Robert S. Rapp, "Josephus and Contemporary Historians" (seminar paper, Grace Theological Seminary, Winona Lake, Ind., 1966), p. 25.

19. William Falconer, "Preface," *Strabo's Geography,* 3 vols. (London: Henry G. Bohn, 1858), p. xvii.

Nabataean guide. Gallus, of course, was prejudiced against Syllaeus in particular and against the Nabataeans in general. This prejudice was passed on to Strabo, who, as Riddle says, ". . . was affected with prejudice of the rank order."[20] Occasionally in his writings, this prejudice very clearly manifests itseif.

Riddle makes mention of another literary work that dates to about A.D. 60. It is called the *Periplus of the Erythraean Sea;* its author is unknown. It does not contain an abundance of information concerning the Nabataeans, but the little that it does contain is valuable. It is of particular interest in regard to the activities of the Nabataeans on the Red Sea. The fact that its author is unknown, however, necessitates the exercise of caution when using it.[21]

Other early literary sources are Appian, Dio Cassius, Diodorus, Pliny, Plutarch, Ptolemy, and Tacitus. Each contributes some interesting information to the study of Nabataean history.

Archaeological

Obviously, this is the more recent of the two lines of source material—that is, as far as its development is concerned. On the other hand, it is the older of the two, in that the materials studied are the products of the Nabataeans themselves. This indicates the importance of this line of study. These remains form the only original link with the Nābataeans that is available to today's historians.

As one walks through the regions formerly inhabited by the Nabataeans, it is not uncommon to find bits of inscriptions, so numerous they are. A vast number of Nabataean inscriptions have come under the study of experts; and as a result, Nabataean epigraphy has opened up to become a significant field of study. A great deal of information about these desert dwellers has been obtained from the innumerable inscriptions that they left behind. Of these inscriptions, many are of a funerary nature; many are honorary; others are dedicatory; and some are architectural.

This epigraphical information has helped in determining their

---

20. Riddle, "Political History of the Nabataeans," p. 25.
21. Ibid., p. 26.

Nabataean inscription above the entrance to a tomb at Petra.
Matson Photo Service

ethnic origin. It seems to be well established that a form of Aramaic was spoken by the Nabataeans, except that this form had ". . . distinct Arabic influence. . . ."[22] Enno Littmann, who has done extensive work with their inscriptions, writes, "The Nabataeans were Arabs . . . their nationality is proven by the large majority of names mentioned in their inscriptions. . . ."[23] Inscriptional

22. Gaalyahu Cornfeld, ed., "Nabataeans," *Pictorial Biblical Encyclopedia* (Tel Aviv: Hamikra Baolam Publishing House, Ltd., 1964), p. 546.
23. Enno Littmann, "Nabataean Inscriptions from Egypt I," *Bulletin of the School of Oriental and African Studies* 15 (1953): 3.

material has been found as far west as Italy; Egypt has produced an abundance of it; it has been discovered in the extreme south-eastern limits of the Arabian Desert, and in the northernmost parts of Eastern Palestine. This situation indicates the extent of their trade connections and their general influence. "The script used was derived from Aramaic and resembled post-exilic Hebrew, except that the letters were much taller, and even in the style of writing used in monuments, some of the letters were connected."[24] Much has been learned about their various deities and their religion in general from their inscriptions of a religious nature.

The longest and some of the most interesting epigraphical materials are papyri found in caves of the Wadi Murabba'at near Qumran. Glueck comments on them:

> Particularly striking is the fact that although these papyri deal with commercial transactions between the Jews, they were penned in a beautiful, cursive Nabataean script by a professional Nabataean scribe. They may possibly indicate that some of the Nabataean clans persisted in their early asceticism and joined with others of similar tendencies. On the other hand, being ordinary business documents, they may merely signify the existence of commercial connections between the two groups.[25]

The latter of the two suggestions seems to be the most plausible. This serves as some indication of the value of Nabataean epigraphy in relation to Nabataean history.

The study of numismatics also provides important information. Often when a new king assumed the throne, he would have a coin struck in commemoration of this event. This has become a valuable method of dating the reigns of some of the various Nabataean kings.

Other types of archaeological remains have revealed much about their culture and civilization. The tombs and temples at Petra, for example, exhibit obvious Hellenistic architectural influence. Dr. Glueck's excavations of the Nabataean temple at

---

24. Cornfeld, *Biblical Encyclopedia*, p. 546.
25. Glueck, *Rivers in the Desert*, p. 199.

INTRODUCTION

Khirbet et-Tannur (slightly south and east of the southern end of the Dead Sea) in 1937-38, yielded a significant amount of information concerning both Nabataean architecture and sculpture. (Much of the material from Khirbet et-Tannur is now on display at the Cincinnati Art Museum.) The excavation of this great temple also was significant from the standpoint of the Nabataean religion.

Khirbet et-Tannur, located south and east of the southern end of the Dead Sea. *John I. Lawlor*

The inner temple court and shrine of the Nabataean temple at Khirbet et-Tannur. *ASOR*

The outer east court of the Nabataean temple at Khirbet et-Tannur. *ASOR*

Surface ruins from the Nabataean temple at Khirbet et-Tannur. *ASOR*

Surface ruins from the Nabataean temple at Khirbet et-Tannur (another view). *John I. Lawlor*

1

Nabataean Beginnings and Early History

The Nabataeans were people of Arab descent[1] who moved into Edomite territory from the south. Their early days are shrouded in mystery. Their invasion of this territory, which took place gradually over a period of two or three centuries, is often regarded by interpreters of Scripture as the fulfillment of the prophecy of Edom's desolation found in Jeremiah 49:16-18 and Obadiah 1:1-4. The language of the Jeremiah prophecy, however, seems to picture Edom as a place of utter desolation after such a

---

1. Opinions differ about this point. The writer for the *Pictorial Biblical Encyclopedia* maintains that ". . . they were not Arabs . . . ," (pp. 542-43). However, the vast majority of scholars believe that they were Arabs. Among those who treat them as Arabs are the early historians and geographers such as Diodorus, Josephus, Strabo, and others. P. K. Hitti takes a moderate position when he says: ". . . they do not appear to us as pure Arabians but rather as sedentarized Bedouins, who, through a shift in many of their old habits, had fallen under the influence of Aramaic civilization." Philip Kuri Hitti, *The Arab Heritage*, ed. Nabihamin Faris (Princeton: Princeton University Press, 1944), p. 36.

fulfillment. The prophet said, ". . . Edom shall become an astonishment: every one that passeth by it shall be astonished, and shall hiss at the plagues thereof. As in the overthrow of Sodom and Gomorrah . . . no man shall dwell there, neither shall any son of man sojourn therein." Such was certainly not the case when the Nabataeans replaced the Edomites. As a matter of fact, that land blossomed forth into a more highly developed and more fully occupied land under the Nabataeans than it ever had been under the Edomites. This being true, the prophecies mentioned cannot refer to the Nabataean take-over. Nor is the time element right. The Nabataeans had already begun to move into this land at least one hundred years before the time of Jeremiah's prophecy.

Two questions need to be considered at this point. The first has to do with the relationship between the Nabataeans and Nebaioth,[2] the eldest son of Ishmael. The second question concerns the identification of these people with the "Nabaiateans" of Assyrian documents. Starcky rejects the idea that the Nabataeans of Petra are to be identified with either of the foregoing:

> From an ethnographical or geographical point of view, the identification raises no objections. But there are serious historical and, especially linguistic problems in the way of such an identification. The *Nabayat* disappear from texts after the seventh century; moreover, the word *NBTW, Nabatu,* of the Nabataean inscriptions is written with emphatic *t* (teth), whereas *Nabayat/Nabayot* is written with soft *t* (taw), and probably is part on an inflectional ending (-at/-ot).[3]

The question that he has raised from the historical standpoint is based on the fact that after the seventh century B.C. they are not mentioned in documents of contemporary nations, particularly Assyrian documents. This, however, poses no real problem; for after Ashurbanipal subdued them once, there would be no need for him to mention them again. The fall of the Assyrian Empire came no more than fifty or sixty years later; this would be further

2. Gen. 25:13, 28:9, 36:3; I Chron. 1:29; Isa. 60:7.
3. Jean Starcky, "The Nabataeans: A Historical Sketch," *The Biblical Archaeologist* 18 no. 4 (December 1955): 85-86.

reason why they would not appear in Assyrian documents after the seventh century. As far as their absence from Neo-Babylonian records is concerned, there was very little, if any, contact between them; so the Neo-Babylonians would have no reason to speak of them.

The linguistic problem that he raises is more serious than the first; but men more adept in the Hebrew language than he see no problem here, for they make the identification between the Nabataeans and Nebaioth.[4] The Akkadian symbol for either "teth" or "taw" is the same.[5] Therefore, Starcky's point cited above (based on the linguistic argument) is not valid. This is not to say that the Nabataean nation began with Nebaioth, and thus existed some 1400-1500 years before their final absorption into the Roman Empire under Trajan. Obviously, being Arabs, they could trace their ultimate ancestry back to Ishmael. But the specific relationship between the Nabataeans and Nebaioth is, at best, inconclusive.

The early days of the Nabataeans have been compared to the experience of the Israelites in that they ". . . took advantage of a vacuum of powers to press into lands more fertile than their own and to prosper there astonishingly."[6] If this is not pressed too hard, there may be some vague similarity; but it should be remembered that Israel's situation was unique.

If the "Nabaiateans" of Ashurbanipal's records are identified with the "Nabataeans," and this writer makes that identification, then their first mention in history would be sometime around 650 B.C.[7] One particular reference to the "Nabaiateans" seems to lend real strength to this identification:

---

4. Francis Brown; S. R. Driver; Charles A. Briggs, *A Hebrew and English Lexicon of the Old Testament* (Oxford: The Clarendon Press, 1962), p. 614. C. F. Keil and F. Delitzsch, *Commentaries on the Old Testament: The Pentateuch* and *Isaiah* (Grand Rapids: William B. Eerdmans Publishing Co. n.d.), vol. 1, p. 264; vol. 2, pp. 412-414.
5. Theo Bauer, *Akkadische Lesestucke: Zeichenliste und Kommentar,* vol. 2 (Rome: Pontifical Biblical Institute, 1953).
6. Nelson Glueck, *Rivers in the Desert* (New York: American Book–Stratford Press, Inc., 1959), p. 193.
7. This date is given as a general date, based on the position that Ashurbanipal's reign extended from 669-633 B.C.

> I inflicted a defeat upon the Isamme', a confederation of
> (the worshippers of) the god Atarsamain, and of the Nabaia-
> teans between the towns of Iaraki and Azalla in a far-away
> desert where there are no wild animals and (where) not
> even the birds build their nests.[8]

This would have come early in their experience in Palestine before the Edomites had completely been replaced and while they
were still nomadic or seminomadic in nature. For many years
while they were in the process of occupying this area they were a
nomadic, or at least a seminomadic, type of people.[9] The complete expulsion of the Edomites by the Nabataeans was finally accomplished by the middle or the end of the sixth century B.C.[10]

Very little is known about what was taking place among the
people of this desert culture during the next century or so. Apparently it must have been during this period that they experienced
a metamorphosis; for when they begin to make their way into
the pages of history at the end of the fourth century B.C., they are
seen as a more developed, settled nation. Kennedy supports this
by stating that:

> After Alexander's occupation of Egypt some of his gen-
> erals twice attacked Petra, about 310 B.C. By that time Petra
> had become a place which could be looted, so that the tribe,
> if originally nomadic, must have altered its customs and to
> some extent settled down.[11]

The change that they were experiencing, however, was not yet
complete. Their later history demonstrates just how much of a
change was yet to take place. Diodorus makes mention of a law
which existed among them yet at this time:

> They have a law neither to sow corn nor to plant any fruit-
> bearing plant, nor to use wine nor to build a house; and
> whoever is found acting in a contrary way is adjudged the

---

8. James B. Pritchard, ed., *Ancient Near Eastern Texts* (Princeton:
Princeton University Press, 1955), p. 299.
9. Glueck, *Rivers in the Desert,* p. 198.
10. A. T. Olmstead, *History of Palestine and Syria* (1931; reprint ed.,
Grand Rapids: Baker Book House, 1965), p. 579.
11. A. B. W. Kennedy, *Petra: Its History and Monuments* (London:
Country Life, 1925), p. 29.

punishment of death. This law they hold because they judge that those who possess things will be easily compelled by powerful men to do what is ordered them because of their enjoyment of these things.[12]

This law demonstrates that there was still a great deal of improvement to be made in their society before they were to become the prominent nation that they later became for a period of approximately three hundred years.

Even as early as 312 B.C. (and probably before), they were a wealthy people; for Diodorus says: "While there are many Arabian tribes who use the desert as pasture, the Nabataeans far surpass the others in wealth. . . ."[13] This also might be some indication that they had begun to settle down and establish themselves as more than nomads. Further evidence of this is to be seen in the desire on the part of Antigonus, a general of Alexander, to subjugate them. This would have been without significance had they still been an unsettled, unimportant people. Two such attempts were made by Antigonus. The first attempt was made by Athenaeus and was partially successful only because he attacked Petra at a time when the majority of the able-bodied men were attending an annual "festival." Athenaeus and his men, being tired and confident that the Nabataeans could not pursue with any haste, set a careless watch about their camp. Diodorus describes the rest:

> While the men of Athenaeus were encamped with little thought of the enemy and because of their weariness were deep in sleep, some of their prisoners escaped secretly; and the Nabataeans, learning from them the condition of the enemy, attacked the camp at about the third watch, being no less than eight thousand in number. Most of the hostile troops they slaughtered where they lay; the rest they slew with their javelins as they awoke and sprang to arms. In the end all of the foot-soldiers were slain, but of the

---

12. Diodorus, *Diodorus of Sicily,* trans. C. H. Oldfather et al., Loeb Classical Library, vol. 10 (New York: G. P. Putnam's Sons, 1933), p. 87.
13. Ibid., p. 89.

The rugged Ras en-Naqb Valley, once part of Nabataean controlled territory. *John I. Lawlor*

> horsemen about fifty escaped, and of these the larger part were wounded.[14]

Upon returning to Petra, they wrote to Antigonus and complained about the actions of Athenaeus. To the Nabataeans, the response of Antigonus seemed to be favorable, though in actual fact he was attempting to give them a false sense of security. He believed that they would accept his response as an indication of his desire for peace. After allowing this situation to continue for some time and thinking that the Nabataeans were by now completely deceived, he sent a second expedition to Petra, led by his son Demetrius. Not being completely fooled the Nabataeans had lookouts posted in high places where they could send signals to Petra if any invader approached. This resulted in the inability of the invaders to penetrate Petra; so the Nabataeans "bought them off" with gifts, slaves, and some tribute money. Demetrius

---

14. Ibid., p. 93.

withdrew and returned to his father. Again, Diodorus speaks of the reaction of Antigonus:

> Antigonus . . . rebuked him for the treaty with the Nabataeans, saying that he had made the barbarians much bolder by leaving them unpunished, since it would seem to them that they had gained pardon not through his kindness but through his inability to overcome them. . . .[15]

Despite their complete routing of Athenaeus and his men, the Nabataeans were not very good fighters. Actually they had not been forced to do much fighting prior to this. It was not a matter of not enjoying freedom; quite to the contrary. They were great lovers of freedom;[16] in fact, this was one of their most cherished possessions. Their best defense, however, was not fighting, but fleeing into the desert. They were capable of existing in the desert over extended periods of time while those strange to the area were not. Probably the best reason for their ability to exist in the desert for such long periods of time was that they had prepared hidden water supplies, which were, of course, unknown to their enemies.

Undoubtedly much of the wealth that has been attributed to them in this early period came through the business of trading. Although full-scale trade operations for which they were famous were not yet established, certainly they had begun to engage in trading on a limited scale. This expanded as their population expanded; and as expansion in these areas became greater, this transformation of their civilization became greater as well. The fourth and third centuries B.C. in many respects were the most crucial as far as the establishment of their culture is concerned. Several of the distinctive aspects of their culture, which helped to bring about its prominence, began to develop during these two centuries. Two prime examples are trade and water conservation.

There was another means through which they acquired a certain portion of their wealth during this period, and this was less honorable than the method mentioned above. They engaged in both piracy and brigandage. Diodorus wrote about such activities:

---

15. Ibid., p. 105.
16. Ibid., p. 89.

Nabataean mural painting from el-Bared. *ASOR*

> . . . after the kings in Alexandria had made the ways of the sea navigable for their merchants, these Arabs not only attacked the shipwrecked, but fitting out pirate ships preyed upon the voyagers, imitating in their practices the savage and lawless ways of the Tauri of the Pontus; sometime afterward, however, they were caught on the high seas by some quadrireins and punished as they deserved.[17]

Whereas this brings out an unfavorable feature of Nabataean history, it also points out their ability to build sea vessels of some kind as well as their ability to navigate them. This continued ". . . until the Egyptian navy drove them from the Red Sea."[18] Hammond says that their indulgence in brigandage followed their expulsion from the sea by the Egyptians.[19]

Before leaving this discussion of the early days of the Nabataeans, mention should be made of what was taking place at the city of Petra. It was much more than a place of refuge when an occasional enemy drew near. By 312 B.C. ". . . the Nabataeans were firmly inhabiting Petra."[20] The Nabataeans were not the first people to inhabit this great fortress city, however. The Edomites, before them, lived there; and evidence has also been found of earlier occupation.[21] Petra underwent some changes and improvements both architecturally and functionally during the Nabataean occupation. Since there was a full occupation of the city by the end of the fourth century B.C., some of this work must have already taken place. So Petra was beginning to emerge as a Nabataean city in its appearance by this time also. More is to be said about Petra later.

---

17. Diodorus, *Diodorus of Sicily,* p. 215.
18. Philip C. Hammond. "Rose-Red City of Petra," *Natural History* 73, no. 2 (February 1964): 18.
19. Ibid., p. 18.
20. Ibid., p. 17.
21. Philip C. Hammond, "Petra," *The Biblical Archaeologist* 23, no. 1 (February 1960): 30.

2

The First Nabataean Contacts
with the Romans

Though they had become a settled, cultured people by the end of the fourth century B.C., they certainly had not reached the zenith of their power. That was to come sometime later. In fact, for nearly a century and a half they made no indelible mark in the pages of history. This does not necessarily mean that during that period of time they suffered a serious decline. Undoubtedly it was a "leveling off" period after having made some great strides toward a highly developed and advanced civilization; at the same time it must have been a period of building toward the great nation that they were to become about a century and a half later. From the end of the fourth century B.C. to approximately the middle of the second century B.C., there are no records of or from any of the Nabataean rulers.

The first king of record during this "new era," as it might be called, is one known as Aretas I. Although not a great deal is known about his reign, there are a couple interesting references to him in history. The first reference to him is found in II Maccabees 5:8. In that context he is said to have held captive for a

37

short time a certain Jewish high priest by the name of Jason who had been expelled from that office by Menelaus. Jason later stood trial in the presence of Aretas and was then banished to Egypt. This was to have taken place in the year 169 B.C., while Antiochus Epiphanes was waging a campaign against Egypt.[1] Aretas I was known as "the tyrant"; and historians are of the opinion that this is an indication that by this date (169 B.C.) Nabataea was already an independent principality.[2] There is one other mention of him in history; it is a short inscription found at Elusa (Khalasah) along the Petra-Gaza road. It makes reference to "Aretas, king of Nabatu." The script of this particular inscription is Aramaic; and according to the experts, the inscription cannot possibly date any later than 150 B.C.[3] If this dating is accurate, the king in reference would be Aretas I. It was probably during his reign that the Seleucids experienced internal strife following the death of Antiochus VII (Sidetes). This situation stymied Seleucid power and aided the rapid expansion of the Nabataean kingdom.[4]

Little or nothing is known about these early Nabataean kings. Following Aretas I, a king by the name of Malchus ruled Nabataea. He is known only by coins.[5] After this Malchus, whose reign is a complete mystery, Erotimus took the throne. About the only thing known about his reign is that whenever he had the opportunity, he marched against the weakening kingdoms of Egypt and Syria. The dates of his reign are given as 110-100

---

1. Jean Starcky, "The Nabataeans: A Historical Sketch," *The Biblical Archaeologist* 28, no. 4 (December 1955): 89.
2. Gaalyahu Cornfeld, ed., "Nabataeans," *Pictorial Biblical Encyclopedia* (Tel Aviv: Hamikra Baolam Publishing House Ltd., 1964), p. 544.
3. Starcky, quoting A. Cowley and F. M. Cross, "The Nabataeans: A Historical Sketch," p. 89.
4. Details of this situation are to be found in "Rome and the Mediterranean" in *The Cambridge Ancient History*, ed. S. A. Cook, F. E. Adcock, and M. P. Charlesworth, vol. 3 (Cambridge: At the University Press, 1930), p. 531.
5. J. M. Riddle, "Political History of the Nabataeans from the Time of Roman Intervention until Loss of Independence in 106 A.D." (M.A. thesis, The University of North Carolina, 1961), p. 34; information taken from the king list in Appendix C.

B.C. In 96 B.C. Alexander Jannaeus became angered at the inhabitants of the city of Gaza because they had invited Ptolemy IX of Egypt to visit them. The result was that Alexander marched against Gaza and lay siege to its inhabitants. Seeing their plight, the new Nabataean king, Aretas II, promised that he would come to their assistance. But before he could do so, the general of the army at Gaza, Apollodotus, was slain by his own brother, and the city was delivered into the hands of Alexander.[6] This is the first of the very few references to Aretas II in history. Littman identifies Aretas II as Erotimus,[7] but there is no conclusive evidence to support this theory.

There is some debate over the identity of the successor of Aretas II. Riddle states that Rabilus was Aretas II's probable successor,[8] while Littman,[9] Starcky,[10] and others name Obodas I as his successor. The weight of evidence seems to favor the latter position. His succession to the throne after Aretas II is supported by inscriptional material. Starcky wrote of a Petra inscription that was ". . . dated in the first year of Obodas, the son of Aretas."[11] This particular inscription speaks of a cult shrine that had been cut out of the rock wall in the Siq. Josephus also mentions this Nabataean king. He tells of the encounter between Obodas I and Alexander Jannaeus:

> . . . but as he had joined battle with Obodas, king of the Arabians, and fell into an ambush in the places that were rugged and difficult to be travelled over, he was thrown down into a deep valley . . . and hardly escaped with his life.[12]

---

6. Flavius Josephus, *Antiquities of the Jews* in William Whiston, trans., *The Life and Works of Flavius Josephus* (1867; reprint ed., Grand Rapids: Kregel Publications, 1964), XIII, 13.3.

7. Riddle, "Political History of the Nabataeans," p. 34. Information taken from Enno Littman's king list in Appendix C.

8. Riddle, "Political History of the Nabataeans," p. 35.

9. Ibid., Information taken from Enno Littman's king list in Appendix C.

10. Jean Starcky, "The Nabataeans," p. 89.

11. Jean Starcky quoting F. M. Cross and G. Dalman, ibid.

12. Jos. *Antiq.* XIII. 13.5; Jos. *Wars* (Whiston ed.) I. 4.4.

Jannaeus had been successful in subduing portions of Moab and Gilead; but it was either in the latter portion of the reign of Obodas I or during the reign of Rabilus, the successor to Obodas I, that these areas were returned to the Nabataeans. Rabilus, also known as Rabb'el, is another of this early group of kings whose reign is virtually a mystery.

Sometime around 87 B.C., therefore, Aretas III became the king of the Nabataeans. He was also known as "Philhellenus." The political situations in neighboring kingdoms set the stage for his entrance into the scene. Riddle describes the situation:

> The Seleucid kingdom, torn by sedition, was in its death throes. Rome was concluding the disastrous First Mithradatic War and a civil conflict was brewing between the parties of Marius and Sulla. The disorder in the Syrian East presented to Aretas an unusual opportunity to prove his abilities.[13]

This Aretas became the first well-known king in this phase of Nabataean history, and his entrance into the pages of history was rather a dramatic one. It should be remembered, however, that the reigns of these other kings mentioned above were not unimportant or insignificant. Though they were in no way spectacular, they did pave the way for ultimate Nabataean prominence, which became a reality during the reign of Aretas III. Shortly after Aretas III ascended the throne, Antiochus XII, the Seleucid monarch, moved against Damascus and gained control of that city; he made a successful expedition down into Judaea; and then he marched down into Nabataea against Aretas III and the Nabataeans. Actually he prevailed over them; but while trying to assist a part of his army that was in trouble, he was slain. When his army saw that their leader was fallen, it fled to Cana.[14] This was the beginning of a successful reign for Aretas III. As a result of this military victory, Schürer draws the following conclusion: ". . . Aretas . . . became from this time forth the most powerful and the most dangerous neighbor of the Jews."[15] Two significant

---

13. Riddle, "Political History of the Nabataeans," p. 35.
14. Jos. *Antiq.*, XIII. 15.1; Wars I, 4.7.
15. Emil Schürer, *A History of the Jewish People in the Times of Jesus* (New York: Schocken Books, 1961), p. 88.

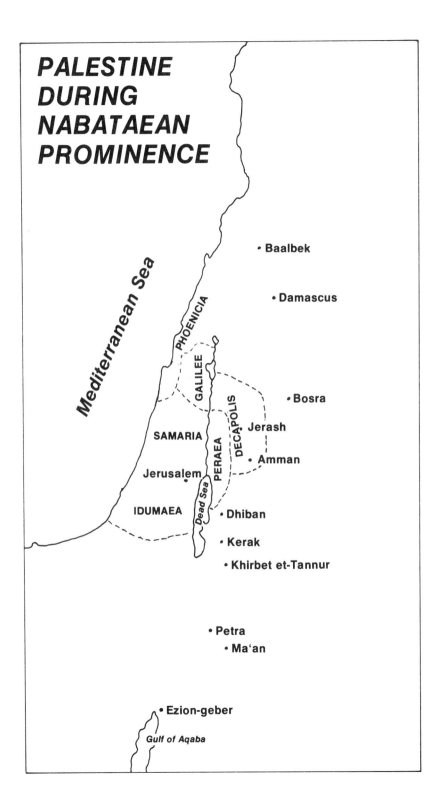

PALESTINE
DURING
NABATAEAN
PROMINENCE

Mediterranean Sea

• Baalbek

• Damascus

PHOENICIA

GALILEE

• Bosra

DECAPOLIS

SAMARIA

Jerash

PERAEA

• Amman

Jerusalem

Dead Sea

IDUMAEA

• Dhiban

• Kerak

• Khirbet et-Tannur

• Petra

• Ma'an

• Ezion-geber

Gulf of Aqaba

events followed shortly after his defeat and slaying of Antiochus XII. The first was the fact that he was asked to become the ruler of Coelesyria by the inhabitants themselves. This they did mainly because of their hatred for Ptolemy VIII (Menneus), but also partially because of their liking for Aretas III. The second significant event was Aretas's expedition into Judaea against Alexander Jannaeus. The expedition was very successful, for he defeated Alexander in battle; but after making an agreement with Alexander, Aretas withdrew from Judaea and returned to Arabia. Despite the agreement that Aretas had made with Alexander (the terms of which are left to speculation), Judaea remained the Nabataeans' main threat.

Aretas III, therefore, was the first Nabataean king to rule over Damascus. Apparently realizing the significance of this, Aretas ordered a coin struck in his honor. It bore the following inscription in Greek: ΒΑΣΙΛΕΩΣ ΑΡΕΤΟΝ ΦΙΛΕΛΛΗΝΟΣ ("King Aretas, lover of the Greeks"). He apparently appropriated this title because of his desire to show respect for a Greek colony that existed in Damascus.[16] Obviously, this cannot be the Aretas mentioned in II Corinthians 11:32.

Sometime between 78 B.C. and 76 B.C.,[17] Alexander Jannaeus died of physical exhaustion. He had taken to drinking heavily, and had contracted a malarial-type disease three years previously, but in spite of this malady had insisted on accompanying his army.[18] Alexandra, his wife and queen, fell heir to the throne, but as Josephus states, ". . . she had indeed the name of Regent; but the Pharisees had the authority. . . ."[19] Being a rather devout person herself, she reestablished the religious system, which under Alexander had fallen into disrepair. Alexandra's reign can be

---

16. Riddle, "Political History of the Nabataeans," p. 36.
17. There is some disagreement over the exact date here. Schürer in *A History of the Jewish People* gives a date of 78 B.C. (p. 89); Boyer, on his "Chart of the Period Between the Testaments" (chart prepared at Grace Theological Seminary, Winona Lake, Ind., 1962) gives a date of 76 B.C.
18. Jos. *Antiq.* XIII. 15.5.
19. Jos. *Antiq.* XIII. 16.1; *Wars* I. 5.1-3.

characterized as successful. In her relationships with other nations she demonstrated ". . . circumspection and energy."[20] She also succeeded in keeping peace at home, and that alone was no small accomplishment. Each of her two sons, Hyrcanus II and Aristobulus II, believed himself to be the rightful heir to his mother's throne. Hyrcanus, being the elder of the two, was actually the legal heir; but as Josephus says, ". . . Aristobulus was superior to him in power and magnanimity. . . ."[21] This situation brought about a great deal of intrigue just prior to and following the death of Alexandra in 68 B.C.[22] Before she died, she entrusted the throne to Hyrcanus. Aristobulus meanwhile had been amassing to himself an abundance of support. It resulted in open conflict between the two brothers and their supporters. Hyrcanus was defeated and Aristobulus took the throne.

While all these events were transpiring in Judaea, Aretas III remained in Petra watching these circumstances unfold and waiting for the right opportunity to move against Judaea. The opportunity was not long in presenting itself. An Idumaean by the name of Antipater, whose father had been a close friend to Alexander Jannaeus and had been appointed governor of Idumaea by him, was a friend to Aretas III. He had taken his deceased father's place by consent of the new Judaean king Aristobulus. He recognized that the possibilities of exploiting Hyrcanus were good if Hyrcanus were to be restored to the throne. He therefore persuaded his Nabataean friends, Aretas III, to give Hyrcanus asylum in Petra and assistance in his effort to regain the throne of Judaea that was rightfully his. After a great deal of persuading, Aretas agreed to aid Hyrcanus in this effort. Probably the final factor that brought about this decision from Aretas was the promise of Hyrcanus that if his efforts met with success, he would restore to Aretas twelve villages on the Judaean-Nabataean border that his

---

20. Schürer, *A History of the Jewish People*, p. 92.
21. Jos. *Wars* I. 6.1.
22. This date may be plus or minus a year. Again, Schürer (*A History of the Jewish People in the Times of Jesus*) places her death in 69 B.C., while Boyer ("Chart of the Period Between the Testaments") gives the date as 67 B.C.

father, Alexander, had taken from the Nabataeans.[23] The towns were important to the Nabataeans because they were involved in the very lucrative bitumen industry.

Aretas did help Hyrcanus in this effort. The records indicate that he put fifty thousand horse- and foot-soldiers at his disposal. It was not long before Hyrcanus moved into Judaea, accompanied by Aretas, to repossess his throne. It was actually Aretas who defeated Aristobulus. When many of the followers of Aristobulus saw the way the battle was going, they seized the opportunity to go over to the side of the rightful heir, Hyrcanus. Aristobulus retreated to the temple in Jerusalem and Aretas combined his forces and those of Hyrcanus to besiege Aristobulus. This perhaps was the very opportunity that Aretas had awaited. Judaea might well have fallen into the hands of the Nabataeans at this time had not a third power from the west intervened.

Pompey, the Roman general who successfully brought Roman power to the East, was engaged in an Asian campaign about this time. In 66 B.C., he succeeded in conquering Mithridates as well as Tigranes of Armenia. He sent his general, Scaurus, to Syria to take care of a situation there. Scaurus came to Syria while Aretas and Hyrcanus were besieging Aristobulus in Jerusalem. Pompey, hearing of this situation in Judaea and not wanting such unrest so close to his activities in Syria, ordered Scaurus to serve as an arbitrator in this dispute. Whether he went to Jerusalem or summoned representatives of Hyrcanus and Aristobulus to Damascus is still a matter of question.[24] At any rate, he met with representatives of both sides. Both parties attempted to "buy" his decision in their favor by offering him a "gift" of four hundred talents.[25] Scaurus arbitrarily decided in favor of Aristobulus. Two questions might be raised at this point: (1) What gave Pompey the idea that he had any right to arbitrate this dispute; and (2) Why did Hyrcanus and Aristobulus agree to allow Rome to decide the question? In

---

23. These villages were Madeba, Naballo, Libyas, Tharabasa, Agala, Athone, Zoar, Orone, Marissa, Rudda, Lussa, and Oruba; *Antiq.*, XIV, 1.4.
24. Josephus says that he came to Jerusalem (*Antiq.* XIV. 2.3).
25. Jos. *Antiq.* XIV. 2.3.

regard to the first question, it might be speculated that Rome found her authority in the fact that she was the superior power. As far as the second question is concerned, it might be conjectured that both parties were confident that Scaurus would decide in their favor. Another point that remains a mystery concerns Rome's atti-tude toward the Nabataean involvement in these Judaean affairs. Arthur Scott, commenting on these events said, "This interfer-ence of the Romans in the affairs of Palestine marked the be-ginning of the end of the independence of the Jews, and ultimately of the Nabataeans."[26]

According to Josephus, Scaurus's reason for deciding in favor of Aristobulus was that the Roman general believed Aristobulus to be better equipped to meet his financial commitment to him.[27] He also indicates that Scaurus felt it easier to eject the Nabataeans than to try to ". . . take a city that was exceeding strong and powerful."[28] The latter seems more plausible than the former, but neither seem to be much basis for such an important decision. Riddle offers a more logical answer:

> As Aretas had already committed himself to Hyrcanus by a costly siege, it would seem likely that Aretas could top Aris-tobulus' offer and make it good. It is more likely that Pom-pey wished to keep a balance of power in the East for the sake of Rome. A decision in favor of Hyrcanus would give the Nabataeans undue influence in Judaea.[29]

With Rome's intervention in Judaea came the first contact between the Nabataeans and the Romans that was of any con-sequence. Just why the Nabataeans accepted Rome's decision is also difficult to understand; nevertheless, they did accept it, and they lifted the siege and headed for home. On their way home, disaster struck. At a place called Papyron,[30] Aretas and his army were ambushed by the army of Aristobulus. For the Judaean king,

---

26. Arthur P. Scott, "The History of the Nabataeans," in *The Sarco-phagus of an Ancient Civilization,* ed. George Livingston Robinson (New York: The Macmillan Co., 1939), p. 383.
27. Jos. *Antiq.* XIV. 2.3.
28. Ibid.
29. Riddle, "Political History of the Nabataeans," p. 41.
30. Jos. *Antiq.* XIV. 2.3.

the ambush was successful; it dealt a crushing blow to Aretas, who lost several thousand men.[31] Apparently this was a retaliatory move on the part of Aristobulus because Aretas had assisted Hyrcanus in his abortive effort to regain the throne.

The following year, 63 B.C., Pompey himself came to the regions of Lebanon and Syria. There he engaged himself in further military efforts, but Pompey's ultimate goal was to move south into Nabataea and, once for all, subdue Aretas III and his people. His plans, however, were interrupted, and he never did achieve his ultimate goal.[32] While in Damascus he received representatives from Aristobulus, Hyrcanus, and the people.[33] He listened to all three parties but withheld any decision. His intent was to deal with the Nabataeans and then return to Jerusalem and set things in order there. Aristobulus, in an effort to work his way into the good graces of Pompey, decided to accompany him in his campaign against Aretas. While still in Judaea, Aristobulus changed his mind and withdrew his assistance. This greatly upset Pompey, who left off with his campaign against the Nabataeans and pursued Aristobulus all the way to the Jerusalem area, where Aristobulus had a change of heart and offered gifts of appeasement to Pompey. This satisfied the Roman ruler, but he sent his

---

31. Six thousand according to Josephus (*Wars* I. 6.3).
32. This is a disputed point. Dio Cassius wrote: "When, then, the regions in that quarter had been subdued and Phrates remained quiet, while Syria and Phoenicia had been tranquil, Pompey turned against Aretas. The latter was king of the Arabians, now subjects of the Romans, as far as the Red Sea. Previously he had done the greatest injury to Syria and had on this account become involved in a battle with the Romans who were defending it; he was defeated by them, but nevertheless continued the war at that time. Pompey accordingly marched against him and his neighbors, and, overcoming them without effort left them in charge of a garrison." Dio Cassius *Dio's Rome*, vol. 2, trans. H. B. Foster (Troy, N.Y.: Pafraets Book Company, 1905), pp. 61-62. Dio's record just does not fit the facts of history; his record reads more like propaganda than history. Appian simply says that Pompey ". . . made war against the Nabataean Arabs, whose king was Aretas, and against the Jews. . . ." Appian, *Appian's Roman History,* trans. Horace White, The Loeb Classical Library, vol. 2 (New York: The Macmillan Co., 1912), pp. 442-443.
33. Schürer, *A History of the Jewish People,* p. 98.

general, Gabinius, on to Jerusalem to take possession of the city. Gabinius, however, met with closed gates and resistance. Pompey became enraged when he heard this, so he threw Aristobulus into prison and advanced to the temple area in Jerusalem where the followers of Aristobulus had taken refuge. Their position there was well-nigh impregnable, so Pompey lay siege to the region. This went on for about three months until finally they made a breach in the heavily fortified wall. A horrible massacre of Jewish people followed. Schürer says that no less than 12,000 Jews died in this slaughter.[34] Jerusalem and all Judaea became a tributary to Rome, the borders of Judaea were greatly reduced, Scaurus became the governor of the new Roman province of Syria, and Aristobulus became a prisoner of war and was taken back to Rome by Pompey. Hyrcanus II became the high priest and ethnarch of the Jews.[35]

Again, there are two questions for consideration. The first concerns Aretas III and Pompey's activities in Syria. Shortly after he became king of the Nabataeans, Aretas was asked to rule Damascus. If Damascus was in his charge, why did he not defend it against Pompey? Perhaps the tie between Damascus and Petra was not very strong to begin with. The other possibility lies in Aretas's realization of the futility of resisting Pompey. Whatever the answer is, Rome took control of Syria. The second question concerns Pompey's original intention to subjugate the Nabataeans before he was sidetracked to Jerusalem. Why did he not pursue these intentions after finishing with the Judaeans? Might it have been because of unrest among the troops? Pompey may have decided that the Nabataeans were not worth bothering with, having a strong desire to get back to Rome. Whatever the reasons, the result was that Aretas and the Nabataeans were saved because of the folly of Aristobulus and his followers. Josephus decried the actions of both Hyrcanus and Aristobulus, saying that because of them ". . . we lost our liberty, and became subject to the Romans, and were deprived of that country which we had gained by our arms from the Syrians, and were compelled to re-

---

34. Ibid., p. 100.
35. James L. Boyer, "Chart of the Period Between the Testaments."

store it to the Syrians."[36] Perhaps it would also be perfectly legitimate to say that because of Aristobulus and Hyrcanus, the Nabataeans were allowed to enjoy a few more years of liberty.

Pompey actually did not delay very long his action against
Aretas. Scaurus, who had been left in Syria as governor, in 62
B.C. made an expedition into Nabataean territory, probably by a
command from Pompey. The results of this expedition are contro-
versial. According to the *Cambridge Ancient History,* Pompey
sent ". . . a force under Scaurus against Aretas; but this commander achieved no more than to harry his territory. . . ."[37]
Josephus, however, gives more detail and at the same time depicts
this contact between Aretas and Scaurus to have been more serious
than the conclusion noted above:

> Scaurus made now an expedition against Petra, in Arabia,
> and set on fire all the places round about it, because of
> the great difficulty of access to it; and as his army was
> pinched by famine, Antipater furnished him with corn out
> of Judea, and with whatever else he wanted, and this at the
> command of Hyrcanus; and when he was sent to Aretas as
> an ambassador, by Scaurus, because he had lived with him
> formerly, he persuaded Aretas to give Scaurus a sum of
> money, to prevent the burning of his country; and under-
> took to be his surety for three hundred talents. So Scaurus,
> upon these terms, ceased to make war any longer: which
> was done as much at Scaurus's desire, as at the desire of
> Aretas.[38]

This account raises an obvious question in the minds of its read-
ers. Was any active resistance offered Scaurus as he moved toward
Petra? That no resistance was offered hardly seems plausible unless Aretas refrained from any resistance in an effort to show the
Romans that they desired to exist peacefully in their own land.
It seems that if the Nabataeans had desired to offer some stout
resistance, they would have been able to do so, especially in light
of the impregnability of Petra. Josephus mentioned the payment

---

36. Jos. *Antiq.* XIV. 4.5.
37. "The Roman Republic," in *The Cambridge Ancient History,* vol.
9, p. 383.
38. Jos. *Antiq.* XIV. 5.1.

Nike-supported Tyche surrounded by a zodiac panel, from
Khirbet et-Tannur. *ASOR*

of three hundred talents to Scaurus by Aretas. Exactly what was the significance of that tribute money? Chapot believed that Aretas, in paying that sum, was "buying his own land"; for had he not paid it, Scaurus would have ravaged Nabataea.[39] He further referred to this as a "nominal suzerainty."[40] Undoubtedly Rome saw it as such also. Mommsen, however, says that, "At this time their subjugation was not accomplished; but it must have ensued soon afterwards."[41] Riddle summarizes the situation accurately when he says:

> It would seem likely that Rome henceforth considered the kingdom of Nabataea politically dependent on the Empire. Also it would appear equally clear the Nabataeans did not feel that the mere paying of tribute or the loss of a skirmish constituted any loss of their sovereignty. Probably they viewed the payment much as an insurance policy. Consequently their policy, while cognizant of Rome, was one of intense independence.[42]

---

39. Vincent Chapot, *The Roman World* (New York: Alfred A. Knopf, 1928), pp. 60-61.
40. Ibid.
41. Theodor Mommsen, *The Provinces of the Roman Empire from Caesar to Diocletian,* trans. William P. Dickson, vol. 2 (New York: Charles Scribner's Sons, 1899), p. 164.
42. Riddle, "Political History of the Nabataeans," pp. 49-50.

3

Malchus II and His Wars with the Jews

The next few years in Nabataean history are silent. There is no conclusive evidence that points either to the end of the reign of Aretas III or to the beginning of the reign of the next Nabataean king. Littman assumes that Aretas III's reign ended in 62 B.C. Since the next sure date in their history is 47 B.C., and Malchus is named as king, Littman assumes that there was a gap between Aretas III and Malchus.[1] There is no evidence to support such a chronology, nor is it necessary to assume that there is such a gap between Aretas and Malchus. It would seem more probable that the reign of Aretas III continued until near the end of this period of fifteen years, at which time Malchus II took the throne.

It is rather strange that the end of the reign of Aretas III would not be commemorated in historical records since he had

---

1. Johnny Marion Riddle, "Political History of the Nabataeans from the Time of Roman Intervention until Loss of Independence in 106 A.D." (M.A. thesis, The University of North Carolina, 1961); information taken from Enno Littman's king list in Appendix C.

accomplished much to improve the Nabataean political situation. The possibility of recovering yet undiscovered inscriptions that would commemorate this is quite likely, however. The fact that the Nabataeans did not have their own historian to record events from their perspective might well explain the absence of any account of Aretas's death from the historical records that have been preserved. Josephus, Strabo, Diodorus, and others would not necessarily have been concerned with the domestic situation in Nabataea. Only as the Nabataeans became involved with their respective countries did these historians have any reason to show interest in them. The fact that there was a "lull in the storm" of political and military intrigue would also explain the silence of the records concerning the Nabataeans. There is one passing reference to them in Josephus, who says that Gabinius overcame them in a battle.[2] He does not indicate who the Nabataean king was at that time.

The first mention of Malchus II dates to 47 B.C., when he gave assistance to Julius Caesar, the new ruler of Rome who had defeated Pompey at the battle of Pharsalus in 48 B.C. At this time, Caesar was engaged in military activity in Egypt, where he met resistance from the supporters of Ptolemy III. Antipater, who "attached himself to Caesar" after Pompey's death, was the "manager of Jewish affairs"[3] in Judaea. Seeing that Caesar was in trouble in Egypt, Antipater appealed to his friend Malchus to lend some assistance, which Malchus did. From all available records, this assistance was rendered voluntarily. If this be the case, undoubtedly behind it was the effort of the new Nabataean king to show friendliness toward the new Roman ruler. If, as Chapot believes, the Nabataeans were subject to the Romans at this time, then this assistance was probably coerced.

During the few years following this isolated event, the situation throughout that entire part of the world became very inter-

---

2. Flavius Josephus, *Antiquities of the Jews* in William Whiston, trans., *The Life and Works of Flavius Josephus* (1867; reprint ed., Grand Rapids: Kregel Publications, 1964), XIV. 6.4; See also Josephus, *Wars of the Jews* (Whiston ed.), I. 8.7.
3. Jos. *Antiq.* XIV. 8.1.

esting but confusing. On March 15, 44 B.C., Julius Caesar was murdered, and the second triumvirate came into being. Mark Antony vowed to avenge the death of Caesar. This left things in a state of confusion in Rome. The very next year, in 43 B.C., Antipater II, father of Herod the Great, met his death in Judaea. A man by the name of Malichus (not to be confused with the Nabataean kings by the name of Malchus) had personal ambition to obtain a prominent position in the government of Judaea. Antipater, however, stood in his way. Malichus bribed the cupbearer of Antipater, who then poisoned his master. Shortly thereafter, Malichus was slain by assassins hired by Herod. Obviously Judaea also was in a state of confusion.

Herod was no stranger to the Nabataeans; as a matter of fact, Herod was half Nabataean and half Idumaean. Stewart Perowne describes the background of this situation; speaking about Antipater, he says:

> It was all-important to him that his connections with Petra should be maintained and strengthened. For the Nabataeans were going from strength to strength. Under their enterprising king . . . Aretas . . . they had expanded northward with successful daring, and had actually occupied another commercial city . . . Damascus. . . . Young Antipater therefore should marry a Nabataean. Negotiations were opened, and since Antipater was rich and powerful, it was with the daughter of one of the leading families of Petra that the match was concluded. The girl's name was Kufra. . . .[4]

Antipater and Kufra had five children—one daughter and four sons. Their son Herod was to become the king of Judaea.

Following the death of his father, Herod established himself as ruler in Judaea. In 40 B.C., the Parthians invaded Syria and moved on south into Judaea. Herod was desperate for help. For some reason—probably because of his father's association and friendliness with Aretas III—Herod turned to the Nabataean king, Malchus, for help. It is rather significant that he should appeal to Malchus for help, rather than Rome. The proximity of Nabataea

4. Stewart Henry Perowne, *The Life and Times of Herod the Great* (New York: Abingdon Press, 1966), p. 22-23.

probably influenced him in this decision. Herod hoped for two things: that he would find refuge in Petra and that Malchus would extend to him a healthy loan. The money was to be used in an effort to reestablish himself in Palestine.

Josephus says that Parthian messengers reached Malchus before Herod; and as a result, Malchus refused to assist Herod on both accounts.[5] Another explanation of Malchus's reaction is offered by Arnold Jones, who believes that Herod had invested heavily with Nabataean merchants who, seeing a chance to keep his money, persuaded Malchus to react as he did.[6] Josephus implies that the Nabataeans had been paying tribute to Herod and that Malchus therefore was refusing to pay that which he owed Herod.[7] If this be true, what was the origin of such a tribute? This, of course, is left to conjecture; but there are two or three possibilities. In 62 B.C., when Scaurus made his expedition against Petra, he extracted tribute money from Aretas III. Possibly the tribute was simply continued. Or it may be that it was initiated at the time of the expedition of Gabinius and the strange and confused circumstances that surrounded that event. Still another suggestion has been made to the effect that the Nabataeans might have been paying a "land rental" on some Mediterranean seaports that they used.[8]

By way of Nabataean messengers, Herod received word of the refusal of Malchus to help him. Immediately he headed for Egypt where Mark Antony was now in control. Malchus, however, had a change of heart. He sent messengers after Herod to overtake and inform him of his change of mind. Herod, however, never received the message because he reached Egypt before the messengers reached him.[9] Undoubtedly, Malchus changed his mind after some serious reflection on the consequences of his actions. Having been refused Nabataean help, Herod turned to Rome, who almost certainly would support Herod. To the Jews and Romans, it

---

5. Jos. *Antiq.* XIV. 14.1.
6. Arnold Hugh Martin Jones, *The Herods of Judae* (Oxford: Clarendon Press, 1938), p. 41
7. Jos. *Antiq.* XIV. 14.1.
8. Riddle, "Political History of the Nabataeans," p. 55.
9. Jos. *Antiq.* XIV. 14.1-2; *Wars* I. 14.2.

would seem that Malchus was favoring the Parthians. But if Malchus really was favoring the Parthians and had intentions of supporting their takeover of Judaea, he would not have allowed Herod to go to Egypt. Riddle's evaluation of the situation seems most likely: ". . . Malchus was trying to stay on the winning side and had made the understandable mistake as to who was on top to stay."[10]

From Egypt, Herod went on to Rome where he sought to engage the aid of Mark Antony. Meanwhile, back in Judaea the brother of Herod, Joseph, along with a few supporters and friends of both himself and Herod, had sought refuge in the fortress of Masada. Immediately the Parthians and Antigonus, the Parthian choice for ruler of Judaea, lay siege to them. The siege was withstood until the water supply gave out. Having heard that Malchus was "repentant" for not giving his brother aid, Joseph decided to attempt an escape to Petra. During the night of the planned escape, however, a heavy rain filled their cisterns, thus rendering the attempt to escape unnecessary. Josephus looked upon this as a ". . . mark of Divine Providence."[11]

At this period of history, the entire ancient world was embroiled in mass confusion, almost as a great forest fire burning out of control. In 39 B.C., Malchus was forced to pay a tribute to Rome for favoring the Parthians over Herod. It was assessed by the Roman commander, Ventidius, who was engaged in a campaign throughout Syria, Judaea, and Arabia. Dio Cassius supports this in his account: ". . . he exacted large sums of money from the rest individually, and large sums also from Antigonus and Antiochus and Malchus the Nabataean, because they had given help to Pacorus."[12] Within two years, by 37 B.C., with the help of Rome in general and Ventidius in particular, Herod had regained control of Judaea and thus became firmly established as king of Judaea.

---

10. Riddle, "Political History of the Nabataeans," p. 56.
11. Jos. *Antiq.* XIV. 14.6.
12. Dio Cassius, *Dio's Roman History*, trans. Earnest Cary, The Loeb Classical Library, vol. 5 (New York: G. P. Putnam's Sons, n.d.), p. 307.

The situation then seemed somewhat stabilized in Judaea, but trouble began to brew from another source. In 51 B.C., Cleopatra ascended the Egyptian throne. This caused no great problem until after Antony replaced the slain Caesar. Cleopatra's great beauty was irresistible to Antony. Well aware of this fact, she played it to her advantage. Political situations then developed that probably never would have, had a man been ruling Egypt. Using her feminine wiles, she attempted to persuade Antony to give both Judaea and Arabia to her. However, Antony could not give to her something that did not belong to him in the first place. Josephus uniquely describes this situation and the result:

> As for Antony, he was so entirely overcome by this woman, that one would not think her conversation only could do it, but that he was some way or other bewitched to do whatsoever she would have him; yet did the grossest parts of her injustice make him so ashamed, that he would not always hearken to her to do those flagrant enormities she would have persuaded him to. That therefore he might not totally deny her, nor by doing everything which she enjoined him, appear openly to be an ill man, he took some parts of each of those countries away from their former governors, and gave them to her. Thus he gave her the cities that were within the river Elentherus, as far as Egypt, excepting Tyre and Sidon, which he knew to have been free cities from their ancestors, although she pressed him very often to bestow those on her also.[13]

Shortly after her acquisition of these new areas, she accompanied Antony on his campaign into Armenia. At this time she met Herod and, according to Josephus, she fell in love with the Judaean king.[14] Herod came close to having her put to death, thinking that he would be doing himself and other nations a great favor. His close friends and advisers however, convinced him that this could only bring trouble upon him from Rome. After consenting to pay her "land rental" for the use of those cities that Antony had given her, cities which actually belonged to him, Herod sent her on her way back to Egypt. She not only exacted rental from Herod, but required the same from Malchus also.

---

13. Jos. *Antiq.* XV. 4.1.
14. Ibid., 4.2.

Apparently Herod paid the tribute for the Nabataeans, who in turn were to repay Herod. Malchus reneged on full payment, however; and this naturally caused bad feelings between Herod and Malchus.

Internal strife rent the Roman Empire, and the course of events became explosive. In an effort to ease his way further into the good graces of Antony, Herod outfitted and trained a group of soldiers to help Antony in the coming struggle against Octavian. Antony refused his help telling Herod to take action against Malchus instead. This in itself was by the cunning design of Cleopatra. She desired to see Malchus and Herod oppose each other, hoping that both nations would be greatly weakened. Thus two former friends now found themselves opposing each other, partially due to the scheming and conniving of the female ruler of Egypt. What followed makes her plotting appear even worse.

Herod and Malchus along with their respective armies met at Diopolis and engaged in heated battle, which was won by the Judaeans. It could not have been a crippling defeat, however, because the Nabataeans reorganized at Cana, in Coelesyria. Herod marched to meet him there, and after a very short delay, the army of Herod again prevailed over the Nabataeans. The Judaeans had the psychological advantage of having already inflicted a stinging defeat upon their opponents. Watching the battle going in Herod's favor was Athenion, a general in the service of Cleopatra. At that time he was commanding a small army that Cleopatra had placed in the area. During his presence there, he had fallen at odds with Herod; so he and his men from a vantage point watched the battle between Herod and Malchus, waiting to see in whose favor it went. Seeing that Herod was prevailing over Malchus's forces, Athenion and his command entered the fray. Only through his assistance were the Nabataeans finally able to defeat the Judaeans; as a matter of fact, it was turned into a complete rout.

Athenion's presence in the area raises a question as to why he was in Judaea and not with Cleopatra, in light of the fact that the battle of Actium was about to take place. It would seem likely that they were there by design of Cleopatra. Being a clever politician, she probably realized that another Jewish victory would

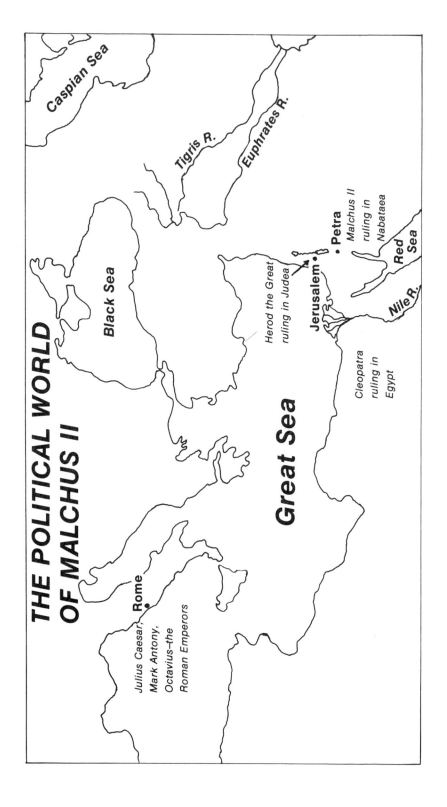

THE POLITICAL WORLD OF MALCHUS II

Caspian Sea

Tigris R.

Euphrates R.

Black Sea

Red Sea

Petra

Malchus II ruling in Nabataea

Herod the Great ruling in Judea

Jerusalem

Nile R.

Cleopatra ruling in Egypt

Great Sea

Rome

Julius Caesar, Mark Antony, Octavius—the Roman Emperors

upset the balance of power in that region. This, of course, would mean that Egypt would have a powerful neighbor, which she could not afford. Cleopatra had instigated the whole affair, but this was a miscalculation on her part. She had hoped that both sides would be weakened; instead, one nation was tending toward being substantially strengthened. By helping Malchus she had hoped the situation could be stabilized; thus, Athenion's presence at Cana.

In 32 B.C., Antony suffered a crushing defeat at the hands of Octavian at the well-known battle of Actium. This led to the end of his power. The Nabataeans, of course, had lent him some troops for this major confrontation; nevertheless, they looked upon Antony's defeat with mixed emotions, for he had been somewhat of a "thorn in their side." After the withdrawal back to Alexandria, Cleopatra believed it to be to her advantage if she disappeared from the political scene for a time. She devised a plan to carry out her intentions; they were foiled, however, by the Nabataeans—the very people whom she had helped. Plutarch records the event:

> Over the small space of land which divides the Red Sea from the sea near Egypt, which may be considered also the boundary between Asia and Africa, and in the narrowest place is not much above three hundred furlongs across, over this neck of land Cleopatra had formed a project of dragging her fleet, and setting it afloat in the Arabian Gulf, thus with her soldiers and her treasure to secure herself a home on the other side, where she might live in peace, far away from war and slavery. But the first galleys which were carried over being burnt by the Arabians of Petra, and Antony not knowing but that the army before Actium still held together, she desisted from her enterprise, and gave orders for the fortifying of all the approaches to Egypt.[15]

This seems to have been rather risky and extreme action on the part of the Nabataeans. What motivated their action? This might have been the work of Nabataean pirates, who are known to have

---

15. Plutarch, *Plutarch's Lives,* trans. called Dryden's, corrected from the Greek and revised by A. H. Glough, vol. 5 (New York: Bigelow, Brown & Co., Inc., n.d.), pp. 236-237.

operated in the area. Or Malchus might have considered the Red Sea his own and took action to prevent Cleopatra from using it. Whatever the case may be, her plan to leave Egypt failed.

After Athenion had come to the aid of Malchus at Cana, Herod was reduced to an occasional robber as far as his efforts against his neighbors were concerned. Much, however, was yet to take place between Herod and Malchus. Late in 32 B.C., Judaea was hit by a terrible earthquake, and the destruction was severe. Both Schürer and Riddle give a figure of thirty thousand people who died,[16] whereas Josephus reduces that figure by two-thirds, to ten thousand.[17] The Judaean army, out in the field when the earthquake struck, escaped destruction. Herod needed help, so he sent ambassadors to Malchus. But in utter contempt for Herod, Malchus seized the Judaean ambassadors and brutally murdered them. Malchus, seeing this as an opportunity to take control of Judaea, immediately moved against the dispirited Jews.[18] Recognizing the low morale of his men, Herod gathered them together and delivered a rousing speech. He reminded his men of ". . . the wickedness of the Arabians, which is to that degree as to appear incredible to all other men. . . ."[19] He reminded his men of Nabataean ". . . covetousness and envy. . . ."[20] Then he told them that:

> . . . if the distresses we ourselves are under, and the miseries that have come by the earthquake, have affrighted anyone, let him consider, in the first place, that this very thing will deceive the Arabians, by their supposal that what hath befallen us is greater than it really is. . . .[21]

16. Emil Schürer, *A History of the Jewish People in the Times of Jesus* (New York: Schocken Books, 1961), p. 134; Riddle, "Political History of the Nabataeans," p. 63.
17. Jos. *Antiq.* XV. 5.2.
18. Ibid.
19. Ibid., 5.3.
20. Ibid.
21. Ibid. The complete text of this speech appears in both *Antiquities* (XV. 5.3) and *Wars of the Jews* (I. 19.4). There is considerable difference in wording between the two texts, but basically they both have the same sense. Riddle comments on the reliability of such speeches: "Speeches delivered by the commander before an army prepared for

The speech seems to have misrepresented a few facts, however, such as the impression that Herod before had continually followed a "good neighbor policy" in his relations with the Nabataeans. Regardless of the extent of its veracity, it accomplished its purpose. The Jews thoroughly defeated Malchus and his troops.[22] In a bold frontal attack, Herod routed the Nabataeans who had left their entrenchment to meet him. Some five thousand men were left dead.[23] Although a comparatively large number of men were able to get back to their former entrenchments, Herod's men surrounded them without delay. The Nabataean army hastily appraised their situation; and when they realized that it was hopeless, they made overtures of peace toward the Judaeans. Herod, however, refused. During the next five days, many of the Nabataeans gave themselves up. Josephus indicates that at least four thousand gave up, while others died from lack of water, starvation, and exposure.[24] Still others tried to escape by slipping through the Judaean lines; their efforts, though, were futile. Any who were left in the trenches were rounded up, and they surrendered. Those remaining acknowledged Herod as ". . . ruler of their nation."[25] Herod, completely elated with his military success, returned to Jerusalem.

A number of questions result from an analysis of the foregoing events. Herod claimed that the Nabataeans were the aggressors and invaders, yet they tried to avoid a face-to-face confrontation. Why? With Judaea demoralized and in such poor physical condition, as was supposed after the earthquake, such a crushing defeat seems unlikely. Perhaps the news of the situation in Judaea had been greatly exaggerated by the time it reached Malchus. Normally, Malchus accompanied his soldiers when they went

---

imminent battle are of rather dubious historical value regarding accuracy of related events. The veracity is to be all the more scrutinized when recorded by an historian not in special sympathy with the general. Nevertheless, Herod's address to the Jewish soldiers is rather interesting for insight into the pulse of the time." Riddle, "Political History of the Nabataeans," p. 63.

22. Schürer, *A History of the Jewish People*, pp. 134-135.
23. Jos. *Antiq.* XV. 5.3.
24. Ibid., 5.5.
25. Ibid.

to war, yet Josephus says that the Nabataean general Elthemus was in charge of the men.[26] This further spotlights the confusion of the days. Riddle offers the following brief analysis of the entire situation:

> His rule being highly unpopular and with the calamity of the earthquake, Herod needed a diversion for his restless army. By feigning an imminent invasion by the Jews' old enemy, the Nabataeans, he could save his position and at the same time perhaps gain a victory. In other words, he yelled aggressor when there was no aggressor. After the raids of Herod across the Jordan, the border army of the Nabataeans would doubtless be strengthened, especially considering the disorder across the Jordan. This army would probably be chiefly made up of local contingents who, after defeat, acknowledged Herod their lord.[27]

Whatever the situation may have been, Malchus did suffer some losses. The first loss was a portion of the Nabataean army. His second loss was that of territory. Just how extensive were his territorial losses is hard to say. Murray and Scott indicate that Herod took over large sections of Nabataean territory.[28] There is little or no substantiation for this extreme position. It cannot be argued that Malchus was not defeated by Herod, but it seems certain that in an effort to make Herod look exceptionally good, Josephus has overstated the facts.

The defeat certainly was not fatal to the Nabataean nation, because life continued on as usual in Petra; nor did they isolate themselves from Jewish affairs. Out of contempt, some of Herod's own people constantly reminded him that in his veins flowed no royal blood and that Rome had given him the position that he presently occupied. Alexandra, the daughter of John Hyrcanus, was thoroughly dissatisfied with Herod's rule in general and with

---

26. Jos. *Wars* I. 19.5.
27. Riddle, "Political History of the Nabataeans," p. 68.
28. Margaret Alice Murray, *Petra, the Rock City of Edom* (London: Blackie and Son, Ltd., 1939), pp. 104-105; Scott, "The History of the Nabataeans" in *The Sarcophagus of an Ancient Civilization; Petra, Edom and the Edomites,* ed. G. L. Robinson (New York: The Macmillan Co., 1930), p. 384.

his treatment of her family in particular. She not only complained but she also appealed to Malchus for help. She sent her appeal in a letter to be delivered by Dositheus, a supposedly trustworthy friend. According to Josephus, Dositheus immediately took the letter to Herod, who told him to deliver it; and if there was a reply, he was to bring it to Herod also.[29] Upon reading the reply of Malchus, in which the Nabataean pledged his assistance to Hyrcanus and Alexander, Herod summoned Hyrcanus and interrogated him about his agreement with Malchus. Whether or not such correspondence was ever carried on between the two is not certain; Josephus seems to call this into question on the basis of "other historians."[30] This, most assuredly, provided Herod with the "excuse" he was looking for to rid himself of Hyrcanus, which he did. Perowne indicates that, "It is out of keeping with the poor man's character that he should have taken any initiative in anything."[31] It was his opinion that Hyrcanus was a victim of the plotting of his daughter, who hated Herod and who still had some faint, but "corroding," ambition of her own.[32] It is in connection with this particular event that Malchus is last mentioned.

The days of his reign were full of adventure, to say the least. Though there is no abundance of it, the reign of Malchus II is substantiated through inscriptional material as well as by coins. Among the ruins of a village known as Sammeh (east-southeast of Bosra) was found what obviously was a door lintel. On it was the following inscription:

1 This is the building which was built
2 by our lord Malik, the king, the king of the Nabataeans.[33]

The village was not of such a size that would warrant the presence of a governmental building; it is believed, therefore, that this prob-

---

29. Jos. *Antiq.* XV. 6.2.

30. Ibid., 6.3.

31. Perowne, *The Life and Times of Herod the Great,* p. 77.

32. Ibid.

33. Enno Littman, "Nabataean Inscriptions" in *Semitic Inscriptions,* Publications of the Princeton University Archaeological Expedition to Syria in 1904-1905, 4th div., sect. A (Leyden: E. J. Brill Publishers and Printers, 1914), p. 27.

The Nabataean goddess, Atargatis, here depicted as the grain goddess; from Khirbet et-Tannur. *ASOR*

Atargatis as the dolphin goddess, from Khirbet et-Tannur. *ASOR*

ably was utilized by the king as a "vacation residence."[34]
A second inscription has been found at Bosra, and it reads in translation:

1 This is the "reserved place"
2 of Mar'al-malik (or: our lord Malik).[35]

This particular inscription has produced a flurry of speculation. If the "Malik" of the inscription is Malchus the king, then this might be his tombstone. It is possible that he might have been buried at Bosra since it was a prominent Nabataean city. Littman suggests that the "reserved place" may have reference to a "reserved seat" in the Roman theater there.[36] "Malik" might then have reference to the Nabataean king or some other prominent personality who resided in Bosra. A problem arises over the fact that there was no Roman theater there during the days of Malchus.[37] Yet another suggestion is that this might not refer to a person at all, but rather to a deity. There was no prominent Nabataean deity by this name, but it might be a variation of the Hebrew and Phoenician god Moloch;[38] or it could have been a personal god of an individual. Littman says that the translation of "reserved place" is literally "secluded place"; but that it might also be translated "sacred place."[39] At best, the whole matter is inconclusive.

Coins of this Malchus have been found, and they bear the following inscription: "Malchus, the king, the king of Nabataea." The coins are silver and have the bust of Malchus on the one side, while on the other there is an eagle with closed wings.[40]

---

34. Ibid.
35. Ibid., p. 59.
36. Ibid.
37. Ibid., pp. 59-60.
38. Amos 5:26; Zeph. 1:5.
39. Littman, "Nabataean Inscriptions," pp. 59-60.
40. Riddle, "Political History of the Nabataeans," p. 52.

4

Nabataean
Achievements

Every kingdom or nation whose history has been worthy of preservation has been remembered because of various characteristics or achievements that made them noteworthy. The Old Egyptian Kingdom was known for its great pyramids and pyramid complexes; Sumer, during the Early Dynastic period, was known for its "temple society"; the Middle Kingdom of Egypt was known for its art and culture; the Philistines were known for their use of iron; other nations or empires were known for various outstanding features. The Nabataeans were no exception. In fact, there were several features that were outstanding about the Nabataean culture. As Glueck says:

> While their turn lasted, the Nabataeans wrought greatly, developing almost overnight into builders of magnificent cities, which are unique in the history of the handiwork of men. They became tradesmen, farmers, engineers, architects and artists of outstanding excellence.
>
> They were a story-book people with almost magical accom-

plishments, which included exquisite pottery, exciting architecture and imaginative agriculture.[1]

This, in summary, is the legacy that the Nabataeans left behind.
It is the purpose of this chapter to discuss a few of these distinctive elements of the Nabataean culture.

TRADE

The success of the Nabataean trade industry was responsible,
more than any other factor, for the economical development of
their empire. In this regard, Baly says: "The immense wealth
which accrued to the Nabataeans from their trade enabled them to
cultivate economically areas which have never been cultivated before or since. . . ."[2] Glueck also attributes the rise of the Nabataean kingdom to their control of the trade routes.[3] As has already
been indicated, their widespread trading also influenced the politics of other nations in that part of the country; and, of course,
through their trading with other nations the economies of those
nations were influenced. Therefore this vast industry had very
definite effects not only upon the Nabataeans themselves, but
upon other empires as well.

How extensive was their trade business? Based upon inscriptions and other reliable archaeological data, it is now known that
Nabataean trade routes went as far north as Damascus; as far
northwest—across the Mediterranean Sea—as Puteoli, Italy, and
the island of Rhodes; as far west and southwest as Egypt and
many of its southern-most cities; as far south as Leuke Kome in
the Arabian Desert and on the eastern coast of the Red Sea; and
as far east as the Persian Gulf. This situation supports Glueck's
statement that "the nation that sat across the trade-routes from
Arabia commanded the avenues of wealth and power."[4] The city

---

1. Nelson Glueck, *Rivers in the Desert* (New York: American Book–
Stratford Press, Inc., 1959), p. 193.
2. Denis Baly, *The Geography of the Bible* (New York: Harper and
Row, 1957), p. 247.
3. Nelson Glueck, "Explorations in Eastern Palestine II," *Annual of
the American Schools of Oriental Research* 15 (1934-35):50.
4. Ibid., p. 50.

of Petra, strategically located, was the center of this vast trade empire. Theirs has been referred to as ". . . one of the greatest trading kingdoms in the Middle East."[5] This, of course, meant that they went overland as well as across the sea.

Trade routes were numerous and branched out in all directions from Petra. The overland trips were made by camel. In his explorations of both eastern and western Palestine, Glueck found evidence of scores of caravanseries. Their frequency along the trade routes would seem to be indicative of the size of this business. What products did they trade, and what was the origin of these products? Many—probably the majority—of the products they traded were their own. There were, however, a few products of foreign origin. In such cases, they served as "middle men"; picking up items of Indian origin, for example, at the Persian Gulf, transporting them overland by camel to the Mediterranean Sea, then on to still another country. Stewart H. Perowne speaks of several such items:

> The Nabataeans controlled the great trade routes from South Arabia, which brought to Petra and to Aqaba not only the spices of Yemen . . . of the Hadhramant and Somaliland, but also the rare gems, woods and beasts of India, the silks of China and the gold and ivory of Africa.[6]

Many items were of domestic origin, and not all of these were exclusively transported out of the general area of Palestine. For example, George Adam Smith indicates that the Nabataeans helped supply Jerusalem with much-needed salt.[7] Like the salt, many products were mined whereas others were produced; and they were in such quantity as to allow them to fill their own needs first and still have sufficient left over for trading purposes. Several industries built around natural resources provided materials both for domestic use and for trade. They might be thought of as

---

5. Crystal M. Bennett, "The Nabataeans in Petra," *Archaeology* 15, no. 4 (Winter 1962): 233.

6. Stewart H. Perowne, *The Life and Times of Herod the Great* (New York: Abingdon Press, 1966), p. 19.

7. George Adam Smith, *Jerusalem,* vol. 2 (London: Hodder and Stoughton, 1907), p. 319.

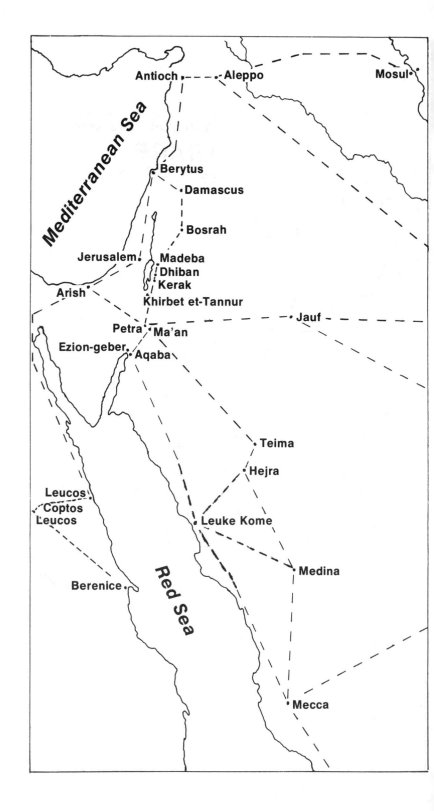

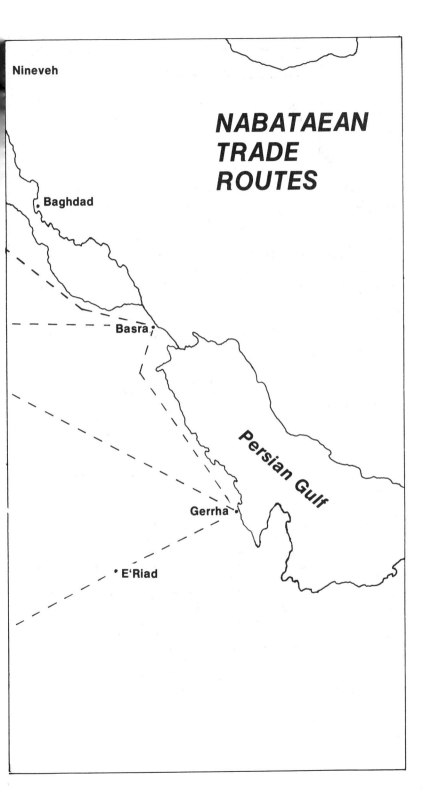

Nineveh

**NABATAEAN
TRADE
ROUTES**

• Baghdad

Basra •

Persian Gulf

Gerrha •

• E'Riad

"feeder" industries for the much larger trade business. Several of these were of such significance that they require mentioning here.

Bitumen

As Hammond stated, "The role of the Nabataeans in this extremely lucrative, commercial enterprise has hitherto been ignored."[8] If the accounts of Diodorus and Strabo are to be trusted,[9] the Dead Sea provided an abundance of bitumen, being the major source of it. Speaking of the Dead Sea, Diodorus wrote: ". . . from its centre each year it sends forth a mass of solid asphalt, sometimes more than three plethra in area, a little less than one plethrum."[10] So large an area did it cover that ". . . its surface seems to those who see it from a distance just like an island."[11] He also described a strange phenomenon that preceded the ejection of this asphalt to the Sea's surface:

> It appears that the ejection of the asphalt is indicated twenty days in advance, for on every side about the sea for a distance of many stades the odour of asphalt spreads with a noisome exhalation, and all the silver, gold, and bronze in the region lose their colors. These, however, are restored as soon as all the asphalt has been ejected.[12]

The Egyptians were the main recipients of this product since

8. P. C. Hammond, "The Nabataean Bitumen Industry at the Dead Sea," *Biblical Archaeologist* 22, no. 2 (May 1959): 40.
9. The accuracy of their accounts have been challenged by "technical experts" (as Hammond calls them). A. Lucas and Warren R. Dawson conclude that bitumen was not used in the mummification processes of the Egyptians, as Diodorus stated. This led to their conclusion that Egypt would have had no great need for the product and would not have been the main recipient of this Nabataean product. Therefore they call into question the accuracy of both records in relation to this industry. Hammond presents evidence, however, which would support the idea that bitumen was used in the process of mummification. Ibid.
10. Diodorus, *Diodorus of Sicily*, trans. C. H. Oldfather et al, Loeb Classical Library, vol. 10 (New York: G. P. Putnam's Sons, 1933), p. 101. One plethrum is 10,000 square feet.
11. Ibid.
12. Ibid., pp. 101-102.

they used it for embalming purposes (see footnote 9). According to Diodorus, mummification would not have been possible without this product:

> The barbarians who enjoy this source of income take the asphalt to Egypt and sell it for the embalming of the dead; for unless this is mixed with the other aromatic ingredients, the preservation of the bodies cannot be permanent.[13]

Supported by a number of sources, Hammond points out a number of other uses to which this bitumen was put:

> There are a variety of purposes to which bitumen was put in the ancient world. The most obvious use was water-proofing for coffins and other articles among the Egyptians. Allied to this is the use of bitumen as a cement or binding agent. This was common in antiquity as a means of joining parts or for tacking. The use of bitumen in fine inlay work and in gilding is not noted in Egypt, but both uses are at least possible there. The Egyptians also employed the substance for the manu- facture of imitation gems, and in the coloring and produc- tion of metals. Bituminous masks for the preservation of mummy faces are cited by Maspero, but are apparently un- common. In the realm of ritual preservation of mummies, scarabaei and amulets of bitumen served to repel enemies from the tomb itself. Perhaps of similar intent was the use of bitumen to obliterate the decorations on cartonage cases, and in cavities behind the mummy.[14]

From the evidence available, it would appear that the Nabatae- ans monopolized this business. This is not to say that the Naba- taeans did not face any competition in the collection of the bitu- men from the surface of the Dead Sea. They did have competi- tion. Diodorus speaks of this competition, as well as vividly describing the method employed in collecting it:

> When the asphalt has been ejected, the people who live about the sea on both sides carry it off like plunder of war since they are hostile to each other, making the collection without boats in a peculiar fashion. They make ready large bundles of reeds and cast them into the sea. On these not more than three men take their places, two of whom row

---

13. Ibid., p. 103.
14. Hammond, "The Nabataean Bitumen Industry," pp. 43-44.

with oars, which are lashed on, but one carries a bow and repels any who sail against them from the other shore or who venture to interfere with them. When they have come near the asphalt they jump upon it with axes and, just as if it were soft stone, they cut out pieces and load them on the raft, after which they sail back. . . .[15]

Obviously this product played a basic and lucrative role in the economy and trade industry of the Nabataeans. It points out another significant fact. "The Nabataeans emerge, therefore, not only as a group of caravaners and agriculturists, but also as the sole entrepreneurs of a basic industry in the economy of the eastern reaches of the Fertile Crescent."[16]

Balsam

The balsam industry was another industry in which they engaged that brought them considerable revenue. This was another natural resource that was used advantageously by the Nabataeans to improve their economy. Apparently they did not use the product to any great extent, but it became a source of revenue by using it as an important trade product. Of course, it was not as big a business as their bitumen industry; nevertheless, it was a substantial supplement to their economy. Diodorus also made reference to this particular phase of the Nabataean business world in his record. He wrote:

> Yet the land is good for raising palm trees in whatever part it is crossed by serviceable rivers or is supplied with springs that can irrigate it. In a certain valley in this region there grows what is called balsam, from which there is a great income since nowhere else in the inhabited world is this plant found, and its use as a drug is very important to physicians.[17]

What Diodorus says points out the double significance of this particular product.

Copper

Still another industry that they pursued and that provided fur-

---

15. Diodorus, *Diodorus of Sicily,* pp. 102-103.
16. Hammond, "The Nabataean Bitumen Industry," p. 47.
17. Diodorus, *Diodorus of Sicily,* p. 102.

ther trading material was their copper mining. Evidence of Nabataean copper works has been found throughout the Arabah. The theory is that they took over much of the Edomite copper industry when they forced the Edomites to relocate. This copper mining, therefore, was not original with the Nabataeans. They simply kept alive something that they inherited from the Edomites, something which had found its origin in the Solomonic era. Some copper mining in this area of the Arabah even predates Solomon, going back to as early as the Chalcolithic period.[18] In certain locations there is extensive evidence of large-scale copper mining operations carried on by the Nabataeans; just two such examples are Hamra el-Fedan[19] and es-Sabrah.[20] That their copper mining added to their wealth is attested by Baly who said that it was ". . . part of the reason for Edomite and Nabataean wealth."[21]

One of the most outstanding characteristics of the Nabataeans was their ability to make use of all available natural resources and turn them into profit-making enterprises. Such ability, of course, testifies to their diversified interests as well as to their capacity to develop these interests. These certainly were not all of their natural resources, nor were they their only tradeable products; but without a doubt, they must rank among the most important.

Incense

It has been suggested by at least one writer that incense was the most important product of the Nabataeans. In his own words, incense was ". . . the main source of the Nabataeans' wealth and importance. . . ."[22] He further states that ". . . their prosperity depended almost exclusively on incense. . . ."[23] It is not to be denied that incense, as well as other aromatics and spices, was an

---

18. Nelson Glueck, *Deities and Dolphins* (New York: Farrar, Straus, and Giroux, 1965), p. 7.
19. Baly, *The Geography of the Bible,* p. 212.
20. Glueck, "Explorations in Eastern Palestine II," p. 81.
21. Baly, *The Geography of the Bible,* p. 212.
22. Thomas C. Barger, "Notes on the Nabataeans," *Aramco World* 16, no. 5 (September-October 1965): 5.
23. Ibid.

important trading product for the Nabataeans. This is supported by early writers like Strabo[24] and Diodorus[25] as well as by more recent writers such as Perowne.[26] However, none of these writers see it as the main source of the wealth of the Nabataean Empire.

The great success of their trade industry was, in part, due to their skilled use of camels when transporting their goods overland, especially when they crossed the desert. Their familiarity with the desert certainly helped to make their trade business successful. They knew the desert like no other people.

WATER CONSERVATION

The Nabataeans' knowledge and mastery of the desert was the key to their existence there. It served both as a refuge and as a residence for them. It was a refuge in times of pursuit and warfare, because they could travel through it with a complete knowledge of it. They also had access to water as they traveled through it; something of which their pursuers knew nothing. It served as a residence to them because they settled down and made it their permanent home and caused it to blossom forth in a way that it never had done before. Naturally, all this required a great amount of water. But in a desert where the annual rainfall was approximately four inches,[27] how could such a phenomenon be accomplished? The answer is to be found in the Nabataean water conservation system. This is, without a doubt, the most amazing aspect of their culture. The success they achieved in this area is no less than spectacular. The rains were few and far between, and they realized the necessity of taking advantage of what little rain they did receive. Consequently, they devised one of the most ingenious systems of water control and storage that has ever been known. If they were to survive and if their vast

24. Strabo, *The Geography of Strabo,* trans. Horace Jones, Loeb Classical Library, vol. 7 (Harvard University Press, 1961), p. 353.
25. Diodorus, *Diodorus of Sicily,* p. 89.
26. Perowne, *The Life and Times of Herod the Great,* p. 20.
27. Ya'akov Morris, *Masters of the Desert* (New York: G. P. Putnam's Sons, 1961), p. 50; Michael Evenari and Dov Koller, "Ancient Masters of the Desert," *Scientific American* 194, no. 4 (April 1956): 42.

trade empire was to survive, they had to somehow make use of practically every drop of rain water that fell in their area. They met the challenge. Hammond wrote of the need for such water control:

> To control and maintain this empire, outposts, villages, and shipping centers, which provided facilities for the provisioning of the caravans, were established. These had to be fed and watered. At the same time, Petra became increasingly urbanized and her facilities more sophisticated, as did those of the larger Nabataean centers elsewhere. This tendency toward urbanization and increased population densities necessitated advances in hydraulic undertakings.
>
> Furthermore, the commercial need for outposts demanded that food production in outlying areas be increased and that the best use be made of available water resources.[28]

They dedicated themselves to this herculean task of conserving all the water that came their way. It was a task that took generations to fully accomplish. Their persistence was not without its reward, though; for this proved to be the secret of their survival. An interesting fact is that all the time they were laboring at this project, all the other facets of their society continued to function efficiently. Their efforts and success in this area have not been ignored by historians:

> They sought out drops of moisture with the same eagerness that hunters display when stalking game. They were motivated by the drive to survive in difficult surroundings and under the most inclement conditions. They knew how to take nature at its worst and make it yield blessings for mankind. Their endless effort, crowned more often than not by success, was to make wheat or barley or grapevines grow where none had ever been planted before and to tap or collect supplies of water where none was known previously to exist.[29]

In this engineering project they achieved phenomenal success. One of the best pieces of evidence that demonstrates their capa-

---

28. Philip C. Hammond, "Desert Waterworks of the Ancient Nabataeans," *Natural History* 76, no. 6 (June-July 1967): 38-39.
29. Glueck, *Rivers in the Desert*, p. 218.

A Nabataean cistern at Bir-Beida. *ASOR*

bility in this task is the fact that many of the cisterns constructed
by them are still useable (they have remained watertight) today.[30]
There were two phases to the system. The first phase was the
catching of water and channeling it into the desired areas. The
second phase was the storing of the surplus. The latter was accomplished through the construction of cisterns that were dug out
of the earth and then lined with plaster to make them watertight.
Diodorus wrote about them:

> . . . since they have prepared subterranean reservoirs lined
> with stucco, it furnishes safety. As the earth in some places
> is clay and in others is of soft stone, they make great ex-
> cavations into it, the mouths of which they make very small,
> but by constantly increasing the width as they dig deeper,
> they finally make them of such size that each side has a length
> of one plethrum. After filling these reservoirs with rain

---

30. Morris, *Masters of the Desert*, p. 58.

water, they close the openings, making them even with the rest of the ground, and they leave signs that are known to themselves but are unrecognizable by others.[31]

The rain water was simply channeled into these cisterns and stored. They had other methods that they put to use in mountainous country. Natural fall-out points in the cliffs were enlarged, and natural basins below were dammed up. In places where there were no natural basins below, they carved reservoirs out of the rock.[32]

Often these were situated so that there was always natural shade over the catchment basins, which aided in slowing down evaporation. Where no such shade was available, they planted trees to create shade.

Terracing was another method that they often employed. This method was used chiefly in connection with agriculture and will be discussed in greater detail under that subject. Finally, there was a system used which remains somewhat of a mystery to scholars yet today. Hammond describes it:

> A final means of water control in these areas is the strangest encountered in either hydraulic engineering or Nabataean history. This is the use of the so-called *teleilat el-' anab* ("hillocks for grapes"). Scattered throughout Nabataean semiarid areas are slopes covered by rows of these small stone piles, or hillocks, sometimes numbering in the hundreds, whose exact purpose—and effect—still baffles hydrologists. Building on local folklore and etymology, some scholars in the field see them as deflection systems, channeling water to the cultivable areas lower down the slopes. In support of this argument, Dr. Nelson Glueck . . . offers air photographs, showing the resultant channels carved by rain-waters—the most likely explanation offered thus far.[33]

The majority of the hills throughout Nabataean territory were lined with channels made out of stones. They were constructed according to the contour of the hill so that the water would run off through these channels to the catchment basins below. It is

---

31. Diodorus, *Diodorus of Sicily,* p. 89.
32. Hammond, "Desert Waterworks," p. 39.
33. Ibid., p. 40.

Remains of a Nabataean dam at Rekhemtein. *ASOR*

Sketch plan of the Nabataean dam and water conservation system at Rekhemtein. *ASOR*

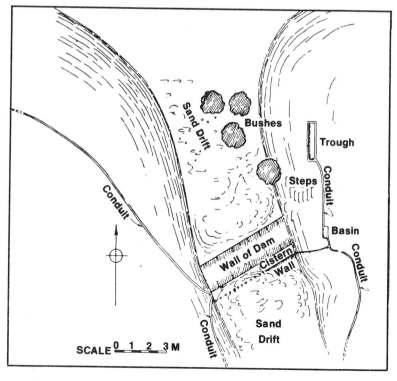

quite evident that the Nabataeans spared no effort and employed every means to capture as much as possible of the little rain they did get. The result was that they never suffered from lack of water. History indicates, in fact, that they always had plenty of water. Many towns had one or two cisterns per house, thus having a sufficient amount of water for themselves; and many towns even provided public bath houses outside the city gates to be used by passing travelers and caravaneers.[34]

For many years, strangely enough, all this work in water conservation was credited to the Byzantines. This situation continued until George Horsfield began to uncover detailed facts about the Nabataean culture. There had been some attempts in this direction prior to the time of the Nabataeans, but these were not as sophisticated as the system that the Nabataeans employed. Water conservation reached its zenith during the time of these highly skilled people. Their influence in this area still is seen today, for Hammond comments, "The modern water control and conservation programs of the Syro-Palestinian area owe a debt to the ancient Nabataeans."[35]

AGRICULTURE

Strange as it may seem, the Nabataeans were very successful agriculturists. They faced two situations that would have seemed to prevent any productive farming. The majority of the land available to them was not of good quality. This, coupled with their very light annual rainfall, would normally have militated against any real success in agronomy. Some scholars have attributed to them just a token of good fortune in this phase of their culture.[36] It is true that in their early days they did very little farming. It, like other aspects of their culture, had to be developed. But nonetheless they did develop it, and it became a major factor in their history. The fact that this was their major source of food indicated the importance of agriculture to the Nabataean existence.

---

34. Morris, *Masters of the Desert,* p. 58.
35. Hammond, "Desert Waterworks," p. 43.
36. A. Negev, "Nabataean Inscriptions from 'Avdat' (Oboda)," *Israel Exploration Journal* 11, no. 3 (1961): 134.

Their large population required a certain level of success in farming. "The country's relatively high level of population . . . meant that marginal lands had to be fully utilized. . . ."[37] Without a doubt, the success in this area enjoyed by the Nabataeans is to be credited to their success in water control and conservation. Baly complies with this conclusion, for he states, ". . . agriculture in such areas was possible only by the most skillful methods of irrigation and water conservation. . . ."[38]

Two different systems were employed by the Nabataeans in their effort to establish agriculture in their land. One successful approach was terracing. Evidence of terracing by the Nabataeans is still clearly visible today; El-Ji, near Petra, is one such example.[39] Hammond comments on the mechanics of this system: "Terracing . . . slowed the runoff of rainfall, and as the water seeped from one level to another, vineyards and groves planted on the terraces retained moisture while providing fruit and shade."[40]

The second method was known as wadi-farming. This was a widely used method. Actually, the Nabataeans employed terracing in their wadi-farming also. Evenari and Koller explain what made the wadis useable for farming.

> Even after a light rainfall a heavy wash of soil-laden water flows from the high ground into the wadis. Its volume is usually so large as to take the form of raging floods, lasting a few hours. The result is that for a few hours each year the wadis become swift torrents of muddy water. Year by year more soil from the hillsides is deposited in the wadis. . . .[41]

When a healthy deposit of this loessial soil had accumulated in the wadi, the Nabataeans carefully terraced them, using stones

37. Gaalyahu Cornfeld, ed., "Nabataeans," in *Pictorial Biblical Encyclopedia* (Tel Aviv: Hamikra, Baolam Publishing House, Ltd., 1964), p. 546.
38. Baly, *The Geography of the Bible,* p. 247.
39. Hammond, "Desert Waterworks," p. 39.
40. Ibid.
41. Michael Evenari and Dov Koller, "Ancient Masters of the Desert," *Scientific American* 194, no. 4 (April 1956): 42.

to do so. Morris renders the following careful description of this intricate system:

> It was converted into a series of terraces, but in a more elaborate manner. Its area was divided into level plots by stone walls and the walls of the central plots served to divert some water to higher plots along the sides. During a rainstorm, all of them became small ponds, so that the water was distributed uniformly. In wadis where erosion had cut channels so deep that control of waterflow by these means was too difficult, the Nabataean engineer-farmers built a series of stout dams to raise its flow so that part of the water would spill over to terraces along the sides. To divert water to still higher ground, they built stone conduits upstream from the dams.[42]

The result of this ingenious system was that ". . . instead of rushing down the wadi the rain water cascaded gently down the series of steps, part of it sinking into the ground at each step and depositing some of its suspended soil and organic debris."[43] A further method of controlling erosion on these terraces was to plant shrubs. Employing these various methods, the Nabataeans pushed the boundaries of agriculture farther into the desert than any other people in this part of the world.

The Nabataeans themselves left records of the great success they experienced in agriculture. Some Nabataean documents have been uncovered at Nessana, which describe the yields of wheat and barley, dates, legumes, grapes, and figs. According to these records, the Nabataean farmers, between the second century B.C. and A.D. 200, produced an eightfold barley and sevenfold wheat yield from each seed planted.[44] The Negev farmers of today produce a nine to elevenfold yield of wheat and barley.[45] Some of the other crops that they raised were olives, pomegranates, and balsam; a great number of vineyards were also kept.

Probably the greatest testimony to the success of Nabataean agriculture is the fact that methods identical to those of the Na-

---

42. Morris, *Masters of the Desert,* p. 52.
43. Evenari and Koller, "Ancient Masters of the Desert," p. 43.
44. Ibid.; Morris, *Masters of the Desert,* p. 51.
45. Morris, *Masters of the Desert,* p. 51.

bataeans have been revived by present-day Israelis in the Negev, and they have used them successfully. In 1956, Evenari and Koller wrote of the experiments being conducted in this regard:

> Up to about 10 years ago the Nabataeans and their agriculture interested only historians and archaeologists. But when the new state of Israel began its attempts to push agriculture into the Negev desert, the Nabataean methods of farming became a matter of highly practical interest. We felt that an intense study of their agricultural system could teach us a great deal to help our own endeavor to recreate fertility in those areas of the desert where the Nabataeans had created it once before.[46]

These experiments were based upon extensive surveys done at such Nabataean sites as Avdat, Subeita, Nessana, and Rehovot. Evenari himself conducted these experiments. Ya'akov Morris records the report of these experiments, which appeared in the January 11, 1961 issue of the *Jerusalem Post:*

> Professor Michael Evenari reports excellent wheat and barley crops and promising fruit orchards at his restored Nabataean farm at Ovdat [Avdat] following last Thursday's one-fifth inch rainfall. Professor Evenari directs rainwater descending from the hills surrounding his 3-dunam (three-quarter acre) farm into Nabataean channels, and had enough water after Thursday's rain virtually to flood his land.
>
> His one-fifth inch of catchment water collected from each of the twenty-two and a half acres of slope and hill totaled six inches on the three-quarter acre of valley floor, produced his wheat and barley, hastened the growth of his fruit trees and filled his empty cisterns, while drought, unrelieved by the same one-fifth-inch rain, killed the orthodox dry farming in the rest of the Negev region. This was the secret of Judaean and Nabataean desert agriculture which has opened the door to the cultivation and settlement of vast acres of the Negev, and perhaps of other desert lands hither-to written off as uncultivable and waste.[47]

Obviously, modern equipment has been used by the Israelis in their reestablishment of these Nabataean farms, whereas the origi-

---

46. Evenari and Koller, "Ancient Masters of the Desert," p. 42.
47. Morris, *Masters of the Desert,* p. 55.

nators of these farms did everything laboriously by hand. Variations have been introduced due to modern technology, but as Evenari and Koller say, ". . . when all is said and done, the best we can do is no more than a modification of the astute and truly scientific methods worked out more than 2,000 years ago by the Nabataean masters of the desert."[48]

POTTERY

It has been stated that "pottery is a very sensitive product of human inventive power."[49] It not only served the everyday needs of its users, but also serves as an indication of progress or lack of progress in a given culture. In the hands of a pottery expert it can prove to be the key that unlocks the door to the establishment of the history of an ancient people. Sir Flinders Petrie once said, "Once settle the pottery of a country and the key is in our hands for all future explorations."[50] The distinctive Nabataean pottery was the key that unlocked the door to the reconstruction of their history. George and Agnes Horsfield, according to Glueck, were the first to recognize and describe the distinctive features of Nabataean pottery.[51] By means of Nabataean sherds, Glueck was able to identify over five hundred Nabataean farming communities in Transjordan as well as literally dozens of villages in the Negev.[52]

What does Nabataean pottery tell the archaeologist about the Nabataean culture? Already it has been pointed out that the frequency with which Nabataean sherds have been found is an indication of the widespread nature of their civilization. It is indicative of another factor, however. It points clearly to the progressive nature of their culture. No "nomadic barbarians," as they were thought to be by some, could have produced this extraordinarily

---

48. Ibid.
49. Ruth Amiran, *Ancient Pottery of Erez-Ysira'el* (Jerusalem: Department of Antiquities, 1958), p. 6.
50. George E. Wright, *The Pottery of Palestine* (Ph.D. diss., John Hopkins University; reprint ed., Ann Arbor, Mich.: Edwards Brothers, Inc., 1937), p. 1.
51. Glueck, *Rivers in the Desert*, p. 200.
52. Ibid.

Bowl rim sherds with typical Nabataean decoration. *John I. Lawlor*

fine, well-fired, highly decorated type of pottery. Hammond quotes R. J. Charleston as saying that ". . . the especial merit of Nabataean pottery lies in its painting."[53] Certainly this was one of the outstanding characteristics of Nabataean ware. Of course not all Nabataean pottery was of this genre; there was some that was more coarse and less decorative. Another characteristic of Nabataean pottery is that it is extremely thin. Bennett speaks of it as being "of eggshell thinness and at the peak of its development akin to the finest porcelain, it is one of the Nabataeans' greatest achievements."[54] One might think that it was extremely fragile, but actually it was quite durable.

---

53. Philip C. Hammond, "Pattern Families in Nabataean Painted Ware," *American Journal of Archaeology* 63, no. 4 (October 1959): 27.
54. Bennett, "The Nabataeans in Petra," p. 240.

86

Small, undecorated Nabataean bowl from Petra. *John I. Lawlor*

Nabataean lamp filler from Petra. *ASOR*

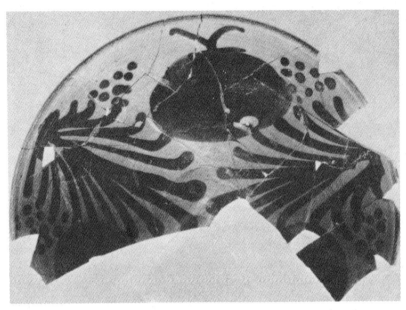

A partly reconstructed Nabataean bowl with typical decoration in reddish-brown paint on buff background, from Khirbet et-Tannur. *ASOR*

A small Nabataean cup with typical floral decoration found at Petra. *ASOR*

A Nabataean jar rim from Petra. *John I. Lawlor*

Decorated Nabataean jar lid from Petra. *John I. Lawlor*

Dr. Glueck presents a description of that pottery that was known as "typically Nabataean":

> Most of the fragments of Nabataean pottery which we found belonged to unbelievably thin beautifully shaped plates, bowls, cups and jugs of various kinds. Many of them were ornamented with painted designs. They consisted usually of stylized floral or leaf patterns in a solid, reddish-brown color, superimposed over very delicate parallel or crisscross lines. Sometimes, leaf and floral designs were most faithfully depicted, and at other times represented a highly stylized form. One of the partly reconstructed Nabataean bowls from Khirbet Tannur [Khirbet et-Tannur] was decorated with pomegranate, palm leaf and date or grape designs in reddish-brown paint on a buff background. Other forms of decoration included bands of rouletting, with the sharp little indentations fitting into each other like rows of diminutive cogwheels.[55]

---

55. Glueck, *Rivers in the Desert,* pp. 200-201.

5

Obodas II
and Syllaeus

Obodas II followed Malchus as king of the Nabataeans. He was not too highly regarded by those who wrote about him. Strabo said that he ". . . did not care much about public affairs and particularly military affairs. . . ."[1] Josephus's opinion was much the same. He wrote that Obodas was ". . . an inactive and slothful man in his nature. . . ."[2] Obodas is first mentioned around 25 B.C., but he probably had become king a short while before that date. He had as his "righthand man" in governmental matters, a man by the name of Syllaeus. Strabo supplies the information that Syllaeus served under the title of "brother of the king."[3] An in-

---

1. Strabo, *The Geography of Strabo,* trans. Horace Leonard Jones, Loeb Classical Library, vol. 7 (Cambridge: Harvard University Press, 1961), p. 358.
2. Flavius Josephus, *Antiquities of the Jews* in William Whiston, trans., *The Life and Works of Flavius Josephus* (1867; reprint ed., Grand Rapids: Kregel Publications, 1964), XVI. 7.5.
3. Strabo, *The Geography of Strabo,* p. 353.

scription has been found that indicates that he was, indeed, the king's brother.[4] He has been described as ". . . a shrewd man, although he was but young and handsome. . . ."[5] He was full of adventure, and this fact brought about many interesting events during the reign of Obodas II.

The reign of Obodas produced two types of coins. The first, known as "Ptolemaic coins," are from the third to fifth years of his reign. The one side carries the impression of the head of Obodas, while the other side bears an impression of an eagle. The second is known as "Attic coins"; they date from the tenth to twentieth years of Obodas's reign. As in the case of the former the one side contains an impression of the head of the king. But on the other side of the coin, the impression of both the king's and queen's heads is to be seen.[6] The same inscription appears on all his coins. It simply says: "Obodas the king, king of the Nabataeans."[7]

As neighbors, the Jews and the Nabataeans certainly had their problems getting along well together. Very early in the reign of Obodas the relationship between the two nations was further strained by the actions of a third party. Zenodorus, a governor from Syria, found that he could subsidize his revenues by indulging in robbery. The area that took the brunt of this less-than-honorable business was the district of Trachonitis, which was under Herod's jurisdiction. Herod protested this action to Augustus in Rome. An arbitrator was sent to settle the matter. The territory of Zenodorus was taken away from him, but he had previously succeeded in "unloading" some of his territory to the Nabataeans for a price of fifty talents.[8] As a result, then, when the land was taken from Zenodorus, the Nabataeans lost that which they had

---

4. Johnny Marion Riddle, "Political History of the Nabataeans from the Time of Roman Intervention until Loss of Independence in 106 A.D." (M.A. thesis, The University of North Carolina, 1961), p. 89.
5. Jos. *Antiq.* XVI. 7.5.
6. George Francis Hill, "The Ancient Coinage of Southern Arabia," *Proceedings of the British Academy,* (London: Humphrey Milford, 1915-1916), p. xv.
7. Ibid.
8. Jos. *Antiq.* XV. 10.2.

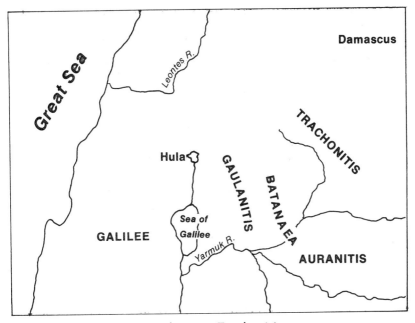

Map showing Trachonitis

purchased from him, as well as the fifty talents. But Zenodorus was fifty talents to the good. The problem obviously had not been handled with justice; so in an attempt to retaliate, Obodas and the Nabataeans tried to stir up a rebellion against Herod. Their efforts, however, were to no avail. This caused no immediate serious problem, but it certainly did further irritate an already uneasy relationship.

Syllaeus made a trip to Jerusalem—the occasion for the trip is unknown—and while there he had the opportunity to dine with Herod. It was at this time that he first met and fell in love with Salome, Herod's sister. Josephus says that she was ". . . very earnest to be married to him. . . ."[9] A few months after their first meeting, Syllaeus returned to Jerusalem and asked Herod for Salome's hand in marriage. Herod consented to the marriage on the condition that Syllaeus become a Jewish convert. This Syl-

9. Ibid., XVI. 7.5.

laeus refused to do, saying that he would be stoned by his own countrymen if he "took up" the Jewish religion. Both sides refused to yield, so the marriage never took place. Riddle makes the colossal blunder of identifying this Salome as the girl who danced for the head of John the Baptist, saying, ". . . if Syllaeus had married Salome, John the Baptist would probably have lived to continue his mission. . . ."[10]

Josephus makes an interesting comment in relation to this situation. A marriage between Syllaeus and Salome ". . . might not be disadvantageous to his [Herod's] affairs, by a union with Arabia, the government of which country was already in effect under his power, and more evidently would be his hereafter."[11] In what sense Josephus meant that Arabia was under the control of Judaea is hard to say. It seems almost sure that Josephus indulged in a little exaggeration at this point; this would not be hard to understand due to the enmity that existed between these two nations. It is not probable that the change in Nabataean kings would have in any way allowed or brought about such a drastic political change. Perhaps in the opinion of Josephus, this dated back to the reign of Malchus II, when Herod defeated the Nabataean general Elthemus shortly after the earthquake had struck Judaea. There is nothing in historical records or in the official relationship between them—such as the payment of tribute—to support this statement of Josephus.

In 25 B.C., Augustus laid plans for an expedition into all Arabia and Ethiopia. At this time the Nabataeans were on good terms with the Romans and, therefore, Obodas promised full cooperation. The purpose of the expedition, according to Strabo, was ". . . to deal with wealthy friends or to master wealthy enemies."[12] Caesar placed Aelius Gallus in command of this campaign. The Romans were completely unfamiliar with the country, so they appealed to the Nabataeans for assistance. Obodas committed a thousand Nabataean soldiers to them, and he "loaned" Syllaeus to them who was to serve as the guide for this venture.

---

10. Riddle, "Political History of the Nabataeans," p. 91.
11. Jos. *Antiq.* XVI. 7.5.
12. Strabo, *The Geography of Strabo,* p. 353.

From the very outset Aelius Gallus and his expedition met with misfortune. The first mistake was the building of large "man of war" type ships. It was a miscalculation because none of the Arabians were well enough equipped to engage in sea battles. This situation was "rectified" by building one hundred thirty ships capable of handling a great load, and they headed for Leuke Kome, which is on the eastern shore of the Red Sea. They arrived after fourteen days,[13] having suffered heavy losses. Syllaeus was blamed for the losses in addition to the fact that he was charged with treachery and deceit.[14] The Roman army spent most of the year 24 B.C. at Leuke Kome. During that year they suffered from famine, disease, and fatigue. Eventually, they came into Arabia where they wandered aimlessly around the desert for six months. It was a dejected, weary group that returned to Coptos in Egypt.

The complete failure of the mission was blamed on Syllaeus. Strabo charged that he [Syllaeus]

> . . . sought . . . to spy out the country, and, along with the Romans, to destroy some of its cities and tribes, and then to establish himself lord of all, after the Romans were wiped out by hunger and fatigue and diseases and any other evils which he had treacherously contrived for them.[15]

Whatever the situation may have been, it should be pointed out that Aelius Gallus and Strabo were friends. This fact, obviously, bore its influence upon Strabo's account. There is more to be said from the point of view of Syllaeus than what Strabo recognized, as is witnessed by this statement from *The Cambridge Ancient History:*

> Its failure was attributed to the treachery of Syllaeus, but the proofs of treachery given by Strabo, who naively reproduces the official version, are mostly proofs to the credulity of himself and his public. While it is impossible to believe that the Nabataeans can have welcomed Roman interference in Arabia or can have generally wished for the suc-

---

13. Ibid., p. 355.
14. Ibid.
15. Ibid.

cess of the campaign, which would have seriously affected their profits from the caravan trade, it is plain that without the services of Syllaeus the Roman army could never have transversed the peninsula from north to south.[16]

Though there were no immediate responses to Syllaeus's alleged treachery or to the failure of the campaign, relations between Rome and Petra became strained. Strabo says that years later Syllaeus was convicted of treason and beheaded because of this event.[17] This particular point will be discussed in another section. Strabo's entire account of Aelius Gallus's expedition appears in Appendix B.

In 9 B.C. Herod went to Rome. The precise purpose of this trip is not known, but evidently it was motivated by political reasons. While he was gone, a band of Trachonites—the inhabitants of Trachonitis, which was north and east of the Sea of Galilee—began to indulge themselves in plundering raids across the borders into both Syria and Judaea. Herod's commanders attempted to deal with the matter, but they met with no success because these robbers were afforded refuge in Nabataea by Syllaeus. From this sanctuary, they proceeded to carry on their raids. When Herod returned from Rome he became furious. Hostilities between the Jews and the Nabataeans resulted.[18] Herod demanded that the bandits surrender, and he also demanded the immediate repayment of a loan that Obodas had secured through Syllaeus from Herod. The amount of the loan was fifty talents.[19] Syllaeus, who by now practically ran the affairs of the Nabataean state, refused to comply with either of Herod's demands. The Romans once again played the role of arbitrator by calling on Saturninus, and Volemnius, governors in Syria, to decide the case. The decision rendered was that Syllaeus was to repay the loan and that subjects held by both sides were to be surrendered and brought to justice.

This situation raises some interesting points. One might wonder

---

16. "The Augustan Empire" in *The Cambridge Ancient History,* ed. S. A. Cook, F. E. Adcock, and M. P. Charlesworth, vol. 10 (Cambridge: at the University Press, 1934), p. 252.
17. Strabo, *The Geography of Strabo,* p. 363.
18. Jos. *Antiq.* XVI. 9.1.
19. Ibid.

about the loan that Syllaeus had requested and received from Herod. There is no record either of when it was procured or why. What little is said about it would seem to indicate that it was made directly to Syllaeus and that Obodas the king had nothing to do with it. It is possible that Syllaeus had requested the loan for purely personal reasons. With the known wealth of the Nabataeans, it is not likely that they were in any financial straits as a nation. The size of the loan would bear this out also. The economic situation in Nabataea was as stable as it had ever been. The suggestion that Syllaeus borrowed the money on his own initiative and for his own purposes is supported by a letter that was sent to Augustus by Aretas IV a few years later. In this letter Aretas charged Syllaeus with ". . . borrowing money in order to obtain the dominion for himself."[20] Another point of interest concerns the personal and official relationships between Obodas and Syllaeus. From all indications, it is to be concluded that Syllaeus, for all practical purposes, had completely taken over the reigns of the government. Obodas had a weak personality, whereas Syllaeus's was forceful. He completely dominated Obodas (who allowed himself to be dominated), and though Syllaeus did not have the title "king," it was he who "made the decisions."

In the settlement of this Judaean-Nabataean dispute, Syllaeus had been given a certain period of time for repayment of the loan. When that period of time expired, the loan was still unpaid, the robbers had not yet been turned over to the Judaeans, and Syllaeus was on his way to Rome. Herod, with the consent of Saturninus,[21] then decided to work the whole matter out to his own pleasing; so he gathered an army and marched into Arabia. Herod found the robbers in a fortified garrison called Raepta,[22] and he proceeded to make an assault upon their position. At this time, the Nabataeans, led by their captain, Naceb, came to the assistance of these fugitives. In the battle that followed, the Na-

---

20. Ibid., XVI. 9.4.
21. Emil Schürer, *A History of the Jewish People in the Times of Jesus* (New York: Schocken Books, 1961), p. 154.
22. Jos. *Antiq.* XVI. 9.2. The site is unknown to historians and archaeologists today.

bataeans were routed, but for some reason the robbers were never taken by Herod. Instead he ceased action against the Nabataeans and returned home. To prevent any further raids, Herod placed three thousand guards (Idumaeans) in Trachonitis. He also made an effort to justify his actions against the Nabataeans to other neighboring nations. This probably was an attempt to gain support in the event that he be called upon to explain his actions to Caesar Augustus.

The Nabataeans made no delay in informing Syllaeus, who by now had reached Rome, of the actions of Herod. Despite the previous situation involving Aelius Gallus and Syllaeus, he succeeded in ". . . insinuating himself into the knowledge of Caesar . . . ,"[23] as Josephus rather cynically states it. As soon as he received the reports of Herod's invasion into Arabia, he made an approach to Caesar. Dressed in black[24] and bearing exaggerated reports[25] of Herod's action, he pleaded for help and justice. His deceitful appeal ended with flattery of Caesar, and strong emphasis was laid on the mutual love for peace that they both shared. Caesar must have been impressed with Syllaeus and, at the same time, angered with Herod. He called forth two friends who had recently been to Syria and were now serving as envoys from Herod. He asked them just one question: Had Herod made such an incursion into Arabia? They, of course, were forced to answer in the affirmative. This enraged Caesar even further, and the envoys were never given the opportunity to explain the true facts of the case. A letter of reprimand immediately was sent to Herod; in it he was told that whereas before Caesar had dealt with him as a friend, he would now be forced to deal with him as a subject.[26]

Word was sent back to Petra concerning Caesar's decision in favor of Syllaeus. There was joy among the Nabataeans in the

23. Ibid., 9.3.
24. Ibid.
25. He reported that 2,500 fine men of his country had been killed in Herod's attack, that his good friend and close companion Naceb had been slain and that they had made off with great riches. Josephus states that ". . . Naceb and about twenty of his soldiers fell. . . ." Ibid., 9.2.
26. Ibid.

realization of the fact that Caesar had favored them, for to be found in the favor of the Roman Empire was no insignificant thing. This also meant that any further action on Herod's part against Nabataea would be sternly punished. The loan was not repaid for some time, nor were the robbers ever returned to the Judaeans. According to Josephus, the Trachonites revolted against the Idumaean guards that Herod had stationed there, drove them out, and continued with their raids in Syria and Judaea.[27]

Herod had indeed fallen into disfavor with Caesar through all of this; so much so that Caesar refused to receive ambassadors from Herod who were sent to bear apologies. The clever maneuvering of Syllaeus had accomplished its purpose—at least momentarily. For a short time he moved ever deeper into the favor of the Roman emperor.

In the latter days of the year 9 B.C., while Syllaeus was in Rome, Obodas II died. His death brought to its end an extremely weak reign. He had been king in name only. It may be that he would have been a stronger personality and king had he not been overshadowed by Syllaeus. Actually, very little is known about Obodas. An inscription has been discovered that lends probably the most interesting piece of information that is known about him. It reads, in English translation, as follows:

1 This is the statue of the divine Obodas, which the sons of Honaimu, son of Hotaisu, son of Patmon............

2 ....(with?) the god Hotaisu, who dwells on the ridge (or hill) of Patmon, their ancestor (?); for the honor of Aretas, the king of the Nabataeans who loves [his] people, and [Suqailath]

3 his sister, queen of the Nabataeans, and Maliku, and Obodat, and Rabel, and Phassel, and Sandat, and Hagiru, his children, and Aretas, son of Hagiru, [his grandson]

4 [in the month . . . . in the ye]ar 29 of Aretas, king of the Nabataeans, who loved his people.[28]

---

27. Ibid.
28. *Corpus Inscriptionum Semiticarum*, vol. 2 (Paris, 1902), pp. 313-315. English translation by J. M. Riddle.

The Nabataean goddess, Atargatis, here depicted as goddess of fruit and foliage. *ASOR*

This one inscription gives information about two Nabataean kings: Obodas II and Aretas IV. The inscription indicates that in the twenty-ninth year of Aretas's reign, Obodas was deified. George Cooke says that it does not refer to the deification of the Nabataean king,[29] but he offers no satisfactory explanation of the inscription. But how could a Nabataean king who did very little toward the advancement or strengthening of his country yet be chosen by the people and the succeeding king to be worshiped as a god? This, according to known records, is the only Nabataean king who was deified. There is no question about the identity of this Obodas as Obodas II, due to the precise identification of Aretas. It has been suggested that ". . . Aretas was so locked in a power struggle with Syllaeus that he deified Obodas to lend more prestige to his succession."[30] This is another of those situations where one can only speculate as to the answer. Whatever the answer is, because of this particular inscription, Obodas II is often referred to as "the divine Obodas II."

29. George Allan Cooke, "Nabataeans" in *Encyclopedia of Religion and Ethics,* ed. James Hastings, vol. 9 (New York: Charles Scribner's Sons, 1928), p. 122.
30. Riddle, "Political History of the Nabataeans," p. 102.

6

Aretas IV
and Nabataean Maturity

Aretas IV inherited an explosive situation from Obodas II. When he succeeded Obodas, Syllaeus was still at Rome and still in the good graces of Augustus. Aretas's real name was Aeneas, but he assumed the name Aretas, which had become a common name for Nabataean kings. Syllaeus was fearful that he would lose his power; so while still in Rome, he sent word back to Petra trying to persuade the Nabataeans to rid themselves of their new king and allow him to be their recognized ruler. Perhaps Syllaeus's message never reached Petra; or if it did, it was ignored, because Aretas took the throne and was well received as the new Nabataean ruler. That is, he was well received by the Nabataeans.

These days of transition were days of strained political relationships. Through Syllaeus, Nabataea was supposed to be on good terms with Rome. Yet Augustus was terribly offended by the fact that Aretas had not corresponded with him prior to his coronation as the new Nabataean king.[1] Rome looked upon this

---

1. Flavius Josephus, *Antiquities of the Jews* in William Whiston,

as a gesture of indifference, especially since Nabataea recently had been favored by the emperor in the recent dispute with Judaea. Syllaeus seized upon this development as an opportunity to try to influence Augustus to remove Aretas from the throne and turn it over to him. So intensely did he want this that he offered money to Augustus. Aretas did finally send a letter to Caesar; this letter has already been alluded to. In the letter Aretas denounced Syllaeus as ". . . a wicked servant, and having killed Obodas by poison; and that while he was alive he governed him as he pleased; and had also debauched the wives of the Arabians."[2]

The letter was accompanied by some gifts[3] from Aretas to Caesar Augustus. But the anger of the emperor had not yet subsided, and he therefore refused to receive either the gifts or the letter. While Caesar's attention was somewhat occupied with the Nabataean situation, Syllaeus was busy on another "project." He hired two assassins to kill Herod; one was a member of Herod's body guard, the other was a notorious assassin by the name of Soemus.[4] The plot against Herod's life was discovered, and the two assassins admitted to their part in the scheme. At this time the political situation in that part of the world was terribly confused and about as unstable as it had ever been during Nabataean times. Syllaeus, a Nabataean, was involved (or had been) in intrigue against the Judaean king, Herod, as well as the Nabataean king, Aretas, and probably Obodas before him. The Nabataen king had not yet been recognized as such by the Roman emperor, and the Judaean king had fallen into disfavor with Rome. Ambassadors and communications from both had been refused by Caesar. It seemed as though Syllaeus had completely fooled Caesar.

The beginning of the end for Syllaeus came when his plot to kill Herod was discovered. Immediately upon finding out about the plot against him, Herod determined to send another am-

---

trans., *The Life and Works of Flavius Josephus* (1867; reprint ed., Grand Rapids: Kregel Publications, 1964), XVI. 9.4.
2. Ibid.
3. Josephus says that Aretas sent a gold crown to Augustus which was ". . . the weight of many talents. . . ." Ibid.
4. Ibid., XVII. 3.2.

bassador to Caesar Augustus. His choice of men was a wise one indeed. He sent Nicolaus of Damascus to plead his case before Caesar.[5] While he headed toward Rome in Herod's behalf, Syllaeus intensified his efforts against Aretas. A few of Syllaeus's supporters in Petra became disenchanted with him and went over to the side of Aretas. They supplied Nicolaus with a great deal of information about Syllaeus's activities against Herod, Obodas, and Aretas. When he made his appearance before Augustus, Nicolaus was "armed" with all this information. His purpose was twofold: he desired to achieve a reconciliation between Herod and Augustus, and he desired to bring charges against Syllaeus.

The day of the hearing came and the representatives of both parties were present; even many of those who previously had been refused admittance were now present. Nicolaus began the session with a series of pointed charges against Syllaeus. He ended his opening statement by saying that Syllaeus was the cause of the alienation between Herod and Augustus, and that all Syllaeus's statements about Herod's activities were lies.[6] At this point, the emperor interrupted Nicolaus and told him to deal only with the matter of Herod's expedition into Arabia following the raids of Trachonitis. The response of Nicolaus was most eloquent and is worth reproducing here as Josephus records it.

> I shall principally demonstrate, that either nothing at all, or but a very little, of these imputations are true, of which thou hast been informed; for had they been true, thou mightest justly have been still more angry at Herod. As for the pretended army, it was no army, but a party sent out to require the just payment of the money: that this was not sent immediately, nor so as the bond allowed, but that Sylleus had frequently come before Saturninus and Volumnius, the presidents of Syria: and that at last he had sworn at Berytus, by thy fortune, that he would certainly pay the money within thirty days, and deliver up the fugitives that were under his dominion. And that when Sylleus had performed nothing of this, Herod came again before the presidents; and upon their permission to make a seizure for the money, he, with

---

5. Ibid., XVI. 10.8.
6. Ibid.

difficulty, went out of his country with a party of soldiers for that purpose. And this is all the war which these men so tragically describe; and this is the affair of the expedition into Arabia. And how can this be called a war, when thy presidents permitted it, the covenants allowed it, and it was not executed till thy name, O Caesar, as well as that of the other gods, had been profaned? And now I must speak in order about the captives. There were robbers that dwelt in Trachonitis:—at first their number was no more than forty, but they became more afterwards, and they escaped the punishment Herod would have inflicted on them, by making Arabia their refuge. Sylleus received them, and supported them with food, that they might be mischievous to all mankind; and gave them a country to inhabit, and himself received the gains they made by robbery; yet did the promise that he would deliver up these men, and that by the same oaths and same time that he sware and fixed for payment of his debt: nor can he by any means shew that any other persons have at this time been taken out of Arabia besides these, and indeed not all these neither, but only so many as could not conceal themselves. And thus does the calumny of the captives, which hath been so odiously represented, appear to be no better than a fiction and a lie, made on purpose to provoke thy indignation; for I venture to affirm, that when the forces of the Arabians came upon us, and one or two of Herod's party fell, he then only defended himself, and there fell Nacebus their general, and in all about twenty-five others, and no more; whence Sylleus, by multiplying every single soldier to a hundred, he reckons the slain to have been two thousand five hundred.[7]

After such convincing oratory, Syllaeus's fate was sealed. Because of the logic and eloquence of Nicolaus, Herod was reconciled to Augustus, and Syllaeus was condemned to die. It has already been pointed out that Syllaeus was beheaded for his treason and his unseemly behavior. It will be remembered that Strabo said that Syllaeus was beheaded for his treachery in relation to the campaign of Aelius Gallus into Arabia. But this was not the case. He was beheaded, but not because of the Aelius Gallus incident. His death brought to an end a period of intrigue and adventure. To him, politics was a game to play for his own advantage. He

---

7. Ibid.

played the game hard, and for several years he won; but eventually he lost, and it cost him his life.

Despite his reconciliation with Herod and the condemnation of Syllaeus, Caesar was still offended by Aretas. Believing Nabataea to be at his disposal, Augustus toyed with the idea of placing the Arabians under Herod's rulership. He probably would have done just that had he not received reports that strife was brewing among the sons of Herod in Judaea. Because of this unrest in Judaea, he decided to hear the ambassadors of Aretas. He received letters and gifts from the Nabataean king, and after reprimanding Aretas, Augustus officially recognized the new Nabataean ruler. Herod was given full authority to deal with the internal strife in Judaea. His actions resulted in three of his sons—Alexander, Aristobulus, and Antipater—being imprisoned and eventually executed. In spite of the internal strife in Judaea—a situation which Herod successfully controlled, and with Aretas happy because he had been recognized officially by Rome, Caesar Augustus for the first time in his reign could feel that his eastern frontier was somewhat secure.

It was into this political situation that another king was born—the King of kings. In light of this political chaos, the prophecy of Isaiah 9:6-7 concerning the person and ministry of this great King, takes on more significance:

> For unto us a child is born, unto us a son is given; and the government shall be upon his shoulder: and his name shall be called Wonderful, Counsellor, Mighty God, Everlasting Father, Prince of Peace. Of the increase of his government and peace there shall be no end, upon the throne of David, and upon his kingdom, to establish it, and to uphold it with justice and with righteousness from henceforth even forever. The zeal of Jehovah of hosts will perform this.[8]

Herod was well along in years; he was suffering from an incurable disease, and finally, in 4 B.C., he died. Just a few days before his death he had named his son Archelaus as king; Herod Antipas was named tetrarch of Galilee and Peraea; and Herod Philip

---

8. The American Standard Version, 1901.

was named tetrach of Batania, Trachonitis, and Auranitis.[9] No sooner had Archelaus taken the throne when a rebellion led by two priests, Judas and Matthias, broke out. After much bloodshed and fighting, the rebellion was quelled. Archelaus then headed for Rome to receive confirmation from Augustus of his rulership. Also, Herod Antipas felt that his father's will had slighted him. Again, Augustus was faced with the responsibility of settling another Judaean problem. While this was taking place in Rome, trouble again broke out in Judaea. Varus, the governor of Syria, moved in to put down the revolt. Aretas, who had been a silent observer up to this point, sent help to Varus. Exactly why Aretas sent this help is not known. Josephus indicates that he had ulterior motives behind his actions; namely, that he did it ". . . out of his hatred to Herod, and in order to purchase the favour of the Romans."[10] To support his point, Josephus cites examples of how the Nabataean army did not wait for Varus but went ahead and burned out Judaean villages.[11] For this premature action, Varus dismissed the Nabataean assistance. Schürer makes no mention of this situation.

The political situation in Judaea became more complex when Herod Philip also went to Rome to support Archelaus and to ask Augustus for more power. Augustus felt the pressure to come to a decision. He decided to uphold Herod's will basically. But for a few minor changes, the kingdom of Herod the Great was officially divided as had been provided for in his will. Archelaus was given the title of ethnarch rather than king. Of the three, Archelaus was the least liked and the least successful. He was tolerated for about ten years before Augustus deposed him and banished him to Gaul in A.D. 6. His territory immediately became a Roman province ruled over by a procurator.

In an effort to heal the wounds between Judaeans and Nabataeans, Herod Antipas asked for the daughter of Aretas IV in marriage; Aretas IV consented. Without a doubt, both the re-

---

9. Emil Schürer, *A History of the Jewish People in the Time of Jesus* (New York: Schocken Books, 1961), p. 158.
10. Jos. *Antiq.* XVII. 10.9; *Wars* II. 5.1.
11. Jos. *Wars* II. 5.2-3.

quest and the compliance with the request were motivated by political reasons. Antipas probably thought it far easier to secure his borders in this fashion than by trying to establish fortresses all along his borders. Schürer suggests that Augustus had persuaded Antipas to enter into this marriage agreement.[12] The marriage was advantageous for Aretas also for basically the same reasons. The name of Aretas's daughter is nowhere given, nor is there any information concerning when this union took place or how long it lasted. Riddle suggests that the marriage took place after the Nabataeans had joined forces with Varus and after Augustus had settled the matter of rulership in Judaea.[13] It is not likely that it would have taken place prior to that time. As far as the length of the marriage is concerned, all that is known is the statement of Josephus, who said that Antipas ". . . lived with her a great while. . . ."[14]

Aretas IV enjoyed a long and prosperous reign (9 B.C.–A.D. 40). During his reign the Nabataeans gained widespread influence. Under him the nation expanded to its greatest size. Coins and inscriptions from his reign were more numerous than those from under any other Nabataean king. Through inscriptions it has been determined just how far Nabataean culture spread. Two inscriptions have been found at Puteoli, Italy, which indicate that the Nabataean influence moved that far west. They also give the dates of their origin. The first one dates to A.D. 5, and reads, in English translation:

1 This is the sanctuary [which]........restored, and 'Ali the copper smith........
2 ....and Marthi, who is called Zubdath........
3 ....Saidu, son of 'Abath, at his own expense, for the life of Harethath, king of the Nabataeans,
4 and of Huldu his wife, queen of the Nabataeans, and of their children, in the month Ab, the 14th year [of his reign] . . .

12. Schürer, *A History of the Jewish People,* p. 168.
13. Johnny Marion Riddle, "Political History of the Nabataeans from the Time of Roman Intervention until Loss of Independence in 106 A.D." (M.A. Thesis, University of North Carolina, 1961), pp. 105-106.
14. Jos. *Antiq.* XVIII. 5.1.

5 . .after the time when the former sanctuaries were built
(?) which Beu-hobal, son of Ben. . . .
6 . .made [in the 8th (?) year] of Maliku, king of the
Nabataeans, they placed within this sanctuary.[15]

The presence of these inscriptions in Puteoli indicates that the
Nabataean merchants had reached this far and had established
a Nabataean community there. The second, which dates to A.D.
11, reads:

1 These are two camels which
2 were offered by Zaidu, son of Thaimu, and Aldelze,
3 son of Haniu, to the god Dushara who
4 heard us. In the 20th year of the reign of Aretas,
5 the king of the Nabataeans who loves his people.[16]

Josephus indicates that the governors of small Nabataean dis-
tricts were called *strategus*.[17] A Nabataean inscription found at
Madeba (sixteen miles southeast of the mouth of the Jordan at
the Dead Sea) bears this out. Without linear distinction, it reads:

This is the sepulchre and the two monuments placed above
it which 'Abd 'obodat, *strategus*, made for Aitibel, *strategus*,
his father, and for Aitibel leader of the camps which (are)
in Luhitu and 'Abarta (?), son of this 'Abd 'obodat, *strategus*, in the seat of their command which they exercised twice
for a period of six years, in the time of Aretas, the king of
the Nabataeans who loved his people. The above work was
made in the 46th year of his rule.[18]

The forty-sixth year of his rule would have been A.D. 37. Still
another inscription, found in Sidon, is significant:

1 This is the *cubicle*, which. .
2 . .the *strategus*, son of Zoilli, offered
3 to Dushara, the god. In the month. . . .of the
4 5th year of Aretas, the king of the Nabataeans.[19]

---

15. George Allen Cooke, *A Textbook of North-Semitic Inscriptions:
Moabite, Hebrew, Phoenician, Aramaic, Nabataean, Palmyrene, Jewish* (Oxford: At the Clarendon Press, 1903), pp. 185-187.
16. *Corpus Inscriptionum Semiticarum*, vol. 2 (Paris, 1902), pp.
183-185. English translation by J. M. Riddle.
17. Jos. *Antiq.* XVIII. 5.1.
18. *Corpus Inscriptionum Semiticarum*, pp. 311-312.
19. Ibid., pp. 188-189.

Obverse of coin of Aretas IV. *John I. Lawlor*

Reverse of coin of Aretas IV. *John I. Lawlor*

This inscription further supports Josephus's reference to these *strategus,* and it also indicates the northern point to which the Nabataean culture reached.

About A.D. 11, the twentieth year of his reign, Aretas acquired a new wife and queen by the name of Shaquilath. It is assumed that his first wife and queen, Huldu, had died. A new coin was struck in Shaquilath's honor; Hill describes it:

> The new issue of coin commemorating the new queen shows on the obverse the bust of Aretas with long hair, perhaps a moustache, laureated, and draped: the reverse shows the busts draped, jugated of Aretas and Shaquilath wearing an ornament of top of her head.[20]

This was just one of many coins that were struck during his reign. Most of them bore the inscription: "Aretas, king of Nabataea, lover of his people." This last phrase, "lover of his people," occurs on all of his coins and inscriptions. For this reason he has been given the title "Philopatris."

In A.D. 14, Tiberius replaced Caesar Augustus in Rome. Not long after Tiberius became emperor, Tacitus mentions that the Nabataean king gave a banquet in Rome at which golden crowns were given as gifts.[21] The Nabataean king was Aretas IV. It is understandable that Aretas would be found in Rome since Rome and Petra were now on good terms. Perhaps the banquet was given in honor of Tiberius himself.

Toward the end of A.D. 28, Antipas had occasion to go to Rome. While there he stayed with his half brother, Herod Philip, who was also in Rome. At this time he met Herodias, the wife of his half brother. She was not only the wife of Philip but also the daughter of a third half brother, Aristobulus. Antipas and Herodias fell in love and planned marriage. Herodias demanded that Antipas first divorce his present wife, the daughter of Aretas IV. Somehow Aretas's daughter heard of her husband's plans to di-

---

20. George Francis Hill, "The Ancient Coinage of Southern Arabia" in *Proceedings of the British Academy* (London: Humphrey Milford, 1915-1916), p. 6.
21. Cornelius Tacitus, *Annals,* trans. Arthur Murphy (Philadelphia: Thomas Wardle, 1844), II. 57.

vorce her and marry Herodias. Without arousing any suspicion, she requested of her husband that she take a little "vacation" in the border city of Machaerus. She was met there by several of her father's commanders who whisked her away to Petra. Once back home, she informed her father of Antipas's plans to divorce her and marry Herodias.

John the Baptist also heard of the marriage between Antipas and Herodias, and he openly condemned it. At the order of Antipas, John was seized and thrown into prison. He was not a long time in prison before he was put to death. The occasion was the birthday of Antipas. Salome, the daughter of Herodias, danced at the birthday celebration, which thing greatly pleased Antipas. Because of her "entertainment," he promised to give her anything she requested. She requested the head of John the Baptist. Undoubtedly, her mother had influenced her in this request. Antipas hesitated to fulfill the request; but because he had sworn to her, he was forced to oblige her.[22]

The marriage of Antipas and Herodias was the event that brought a great deal of trouble to Antipas. Aretas became extremely angry—probably not so much over the marriage as over the unjust treatment of his daughter by Antipas. Consequently, both sides prepared for war. Neither king went to war himself; rather, they both left matters in the charge of their generals. They joined battle, and the Judaeans were thoroughly defeated. The defeat of Antipas's army has been blamed on the fact that many Jews deserted Antipas's side and went over to the Nabataeans. Josephus says that those who did so were of the tetrarchy of Philip.[23] He goes on to point out that many Jews believed the defeat of the Jewish army to be the result of "Divine Providence," which brought the defeat upon Antipas as punishment for the execution of John the Baptist.[24]

About this time (circ. A.D. 30) Jesus, the true King of the Jews, was put to death at Jerusalem. The Jews often had appealed to Rome to bring about peace in the midst of all the political

---

22. Matt. 14:1-12; Mark 6:16-29.
23. Jos. *Antiq.* XVIII. 5.1.
24. Ibid., 5.2.

chaos of their day. Yet when the true King of the Jews—the Prince of Peace—came, they rejected Him. This makes the sign that Pilate had placed on the cross stand forth in exceedingly bold letters: "JESUS THE NAZARENE: THE KING OF THE JEWS."[25]

When Tiberius received the news of the Nabataean victory, he sent urgent orders to Vitellius, the governor of Syria, that he was ". . . to make war upon him [Aretas], and either to take him alive, and bring him in bonds, or to kill him, and send him his head."[26] It seems strange that this one incident should cause Tiberius to resort to such drastic measures. Perhaps this afforded the Roman emperor the long-sought opportunity to subjugate the Nabataeans once for all.

Vitellius prepared for a march against Aretas. He took with him two legions of armed men—those of "light armature" and horsemen.[27] When Aretas heard that Vitellius was on his way, he consulted his personal diviners and then boasted that it was impossible for Vitellius's army to enter Petra. He indicated that one of the two rulers would die.[28] Vitellius began his march toward Nabataea. His march took him though Judaea. The Jewish people resented the presence of this army in their land, and they requested Vitellius to take another route to Nabataea, Josephus again supplies the reason for this request: ". . . the laws of their country would not permit them to overlook those images which were brought into it, of which there were a great many in their ensigns. . . ."[29] Vitellius yielded to their request; he commanded his troops to take another route although he went to Jerusalem as Herod Antipas's guest of honor. While there, he received word from Rome of the death Tiberius. He believed that this turn of events relieved him of his responsibilities toward the Nabataeans; he withdrew his army and returned to Syria.

---

25. John 19:19, New American Standard Bible—New Testament. See also Matt. 27:37; Mark 15:26; and Luke 23:38.
26. Jos. *Antiq.* XVIII. 5.1.
27. Ibid., 5.3.
28. Ibid.
29. Ibid.

Schürer indicates that this took place in March, A.D. 37.[30] It is tempting to speculate on the outcome of such a clash as that between Vitellius and Aretas. That it undoubtedly would have taken place near Petra would have given the Nabataeans somewhat of an advantage. But Tiberius, who was determined to bring about the end of Nabataean independence, would have stopped short of nothing. Because of the death of Tiberius, however, Aretas and the Nabataeans were spared.

At this point it is necessary to backtrack a few years to late A.D. 34 or early 35. Paul was in Damascus when the Jews of that city made an attempt on his life. He has recorded that incident in II Corinthians 11:32-33: "In Damascus the ethnarch under Aretas the king was guarding the city of the Damascenes in order to seize me, and I was let down in a basket through a window in the wall, and so escaped his hand."[31] The question concerns the presence of a Nabataean ethnarch in Damascus at that date. The Aretas that Paul mentions is without a doubt Aretas IV. Back about 85 B.C., Aretas III was mentioned as being ruler in Damascus, but shortly thereafter Rome took control of Syria; and Nabataean control is never again mentioned except for this one reference. Various solutions have been offered. Rev. E. H. Plumptre, writing for *Ellicott's Commentary,* wrote:

> It is probable . . . that in the war which Aretas had declared against Herod Antipas, in consequence of the Tetrarch's divorcing his daughter in order that he might marry Herodias . . . he had been led, after defeating the Tetrarch . . . to push his victories farther; and, taking advantage of the absence of Vitelius, who had hastened to Rome on hearing of the death of Tiberius (A.D. 37) had seized on Damascus. In this abeyance of the control of the Roman power, Aretas may have desired to conciliate the priestly part at Jerusalem by giving facilities to their action against the sect which they would naturally represent as identified with the Galileans against whom he had been waging war.[32]

---

30. Schürer, *A History of the Jewish People,* p. 173.
31. New American Standard Bible—New Testament. See Luke's account of this incident in Acts 9:23-25.
32. E. H. Plumptre, "The Acts of the Apostles" in *Ellicott's Commentary on the Whole Bible,* ed. Charles John Ellicott, vols. 7, 8 (Grand Rapids: Zondervan Publishing House, 1959 reprint), p. 56.

The head of the Nabataean god, Zeus-Hadad, from Khirbet et-Tannur. *ASOR*

This view was also held by Adam Clarke.[33] If this be the solution, then Nabataean control at this time could only have been but for a very short time. Schürer believed that Damascus was restored to the Nabataeans as an apology by Caligula because of Vitellius's expedition.[34] Littman simply believes that the Nabataeans controlled Damascus during the years A.D. 30-40.[35] If this be true, then how is the presence of Vitellius in Syria (as governor) accounted for? Mommsen offers this lengthy solution:

---

33. Adam Clarke, "Second Epistle to the Corinthians" in *Clarke's Commentary,* vol. 6 (New York: Abingdon-Cokesbury Press, n.d.), p. 365.
34. Schürer, *A History of the Jewish People in the Time of Jesus,* cited by Riddle, "Political History of the Nabataeans," p. 117.
35. Enno Littman, "Nabataean Inscriptions" in *Semitic Inscriptions.* Publications of the Princeton University Archaeological Expedition to Syria in 1904-1905, 4th div., sect. A (Leyden: E. J. Brill Publishers and Printers, 1914), p. xi.

Probably this dependence of the city on the Nabataean kings subsisted so long as there were such kings. . . . The continuance of the Nabataean rule is attested partly by the circumstance that the ethnarch of king Aretas in Damascus wished to have the Apostle Paul arrested, as the latter writes in II Corinthians 11:32, partly by the recently-established fact that the rule of the Nabataeans to the northeast of Damascus was still continuing under Trajan. Those who start . . . from the view that, if Aretas ruled in Damascus, the city could not be Roman, have attempted in various ways to fix the chronology of that event in the life of Paul. They have thought of the complication between Aretas and the Roman government in the last years of Tiberius; but from the course which this took it is not probable that it brought about a permanent change in the state of possession of Aretas. Melchoir de Vogue' . . . has pointed out that between Tiberius and Nero—more precisely, between the years 33 and 62 . . . there are no imperial coins of Damascus, and has placed the rule of the Nabataeans there in this interval, on the assumption that the emperor Gaius showed his favor to the Arabian as to so many others of the vassal-princes, and invested him with Damascus. But such interruptions of coinage are of frequent occurrence, and require no such profound explanation.[36]

Involved in this problem is the meaning of the term "ethnarch" (ἐθνάρχης). Clarke simply says: "The word *ethnarch* signifies the governor of a province, under a king or emperor."[37] Arndt and Gingrich agree with this meaning.[38] Another idea, but not acceptable, is that in this case the "ethnarch" of Aretas was a Bedouin chief who watched the city gates. Lenski takes this view when he says, "We think of this Ethnarch as an Arabian sheik."[39]

---

36. Theodor Mommsen, *The Provinces of the Roman Empire from Caesar to Diocletian,* trans. William P. Dickson, vol. 2 (New York: Charles Scribner's Sons, 1899), pp. 162-164.
37. Clarke, "Second Epistle to the Corinthians," p. 365.
38. W. R. Arndt and F. W. Gingrich, *A Greek-English Lexicon of the New Testament and Other Early Christian Literature* (Chicago: The University of Chicago Press, 1957), p. 217.
39. R. C. H. Lenski, *The Interpretation of I and II Corinthians* (Minneapolis: Augsburg Publishing House, 1937), p. 1289.

The question involving Damascus seems to be incapable of being completely resolved. Unfortunately there are neither coins nor inscriptions to help solve the problem. Starcky's closing statement on the matter sums it all up: "The question remains open."[40]

After Tiberius died in A.D. 37, Caligula replaced him as emperor of Rome. The rest of the reign of Aretas IV apparently passed by peacefully and without any events of real consequence. His reign turned out to be the period when the Nabataeans achieved their greatest prominence. He lived a long life, and he ruled his nation well.

---

40. Jean Starcky, "The Nabataeans: A Historical Sketch," *The Biblical Archaeologist* 18, no. 4 (December 1955): 98.

7

The Last Nabataean Kings and Annexation

Existing records of the last years of the Nabataeans are not clear. The Nabataean civilization reached its zenith under Aretas IV, and the evidence does indicate that this level was maintained for several years, even after Aretas had passed from the scene. There is some question as to who succeeded Aretas in Petra. Josephus speaks of Abia, the king of the Arabians.[1] He makes reference to him in relation to Izates, the king of the Abiabeneans —a nation east of the Euphrates. Izates apparently became a Jewish convert, which caused his people to hate him greatly. Soon the brother of Izates, along with other leaders, followed the example of his brother and their king. The Abiabeneans determined to "punish" their leaders for defecting from their native religion. They contacted Abia and promised a great amount of money to him if he would move against Izates. They further indicated

---

1. Flavius Josephus, *Antiquities of the Jews* in William Whiston, trans., *The Life and Times of Flavius Josephus* (1867; reprint ed., Grand Rapids: Kregel Publications, 1964), XX. 4.1.

that upon first contact between the two armies, they would desert to Abia. The amount of money that was promised is not known, but it must have been a very large amount because Abia accepted the offer. Money could have been the only motive for Nabataean involvement in this affair, for they had had no previous contacts with these people. A large Nabataean army moved into Abia-bene and engaged Izates in battle. Those who had promised Abia that they would desert, did, but Izates did not become disheartened when he learned who the deserters were. He successfully withdrew into a safe place and posthaste executed all the traitors. The next day, with renewed vigor, he again met the Nabataeans. This time, however, Abia and his men were put to flight by Izates and his army. They took refuge in a fortress known as Arsamus,[2] to which Izates immediately laid siege. Then followed something that was not before known in Nabataean history. Abia saw the futility of his position, and not wanting to suffer the humility of being taken alive, he slew himself with his sword. He was the first and only Nabataean king (?) to die as a result of hostilities.

Doubt has been cast on the existence of a Nabataean king called Abia. Many, probably the majority, of king lists do not include him. There are no extant inscriptions or coins that testify of his alleged reign, but this in itself is not conclusive evidence. Perhaps Abia was a governmental administrator and general, similar to Syllaeus, serving under Malchus III.

Archaeological evidence of Malchus's reign is abundant. Assuming Malchus III to be the successor to Aretas IV, he then began his reign in A.D. 40, and it continued until A.D. 70/71. Just after he took the throne in Petra, there was a change of rulers in Rome; Caligula's short reign came to an end, and Claudius replaced him. Other than his reference to Abia and his encounter with Izates, Josephus's only reference to the Nabataeans during the days of Claudius is where he mentions them along with the Idumaeans as being the objects of abuse at the hands of the rich and successful robber, Tholomy.[3]

---

2. Ibid.
3. Ibid., 1.1.

On the Judaean-Nabataean front, the situation apparently remained stable during Malchus's reign. The constant conflict that had plagued them in previous days was absent. Probably this is to be attributed to the fact that the situation in Judaea was building up to what was to end in the destruction of Jerusalem in A.D. 70. Judaea was too busy with her own affairs to get involved with the Nabataeans.

The only literary reference to Malchus III is found in Josephus. In A.D. 67, Titus arrived in Alexandria to form his army for the coming Jewish campaign. Aid was forthcoming from many regions of the East to assist Rome in the slaughter of the Jews. Malchus gave his help also. Josephus indicates that he sent a thousand horsemen and five thousand foot soldiers, the majority of which were archers.[4]

The following interesting Nabataean inscription was found at Salhad:

1 This is the temple which Ruhu, son of Malike, son of Aklabu, son of Ruhri, built to Allat, their goddess,
2 who is in Salhad, whom Ruhu, son of Zaisu with the above designated Ruhu had established.
3 In the month Ab in the 17th year of Malchus, the king of the Nabataeans, son of Aretas, the king of the Nabataeans who loved his people.[5]

This inscription dates to the seventeenth year of Malchus's reign, or A.D. 57. It is interesting to note that Aretas IV, even after his death, still was known as the Nabataean king who loved his people.

Littman offers another inscription as one belonging to Malchus III. Its translation reads:

1 This is the cult-stone
2 which was made
3 by 'Ubaid, the son
4 of 'Utafik (?)
5 for Ba'al-Shamin, the god

---

4. Jos. *Wars of the Jews* (Whiston ed.), III. 4.2.
5. *Corpus Inscriptionum Semiticarum*, vol. 2 (Paris, 1902), pp. 192-193. English translations by J. M. Riddle.

6 of Matan (?) in the year
7 33 of Malik
8 the king, the king of the Nabataeans.[6]

This one, however, poses a problem in that the inscription dates to A.D. 73; but Rabilus (Rabbel) II became king no later than A.D. 71.[7] It is possible that this is an inscription belonging to the first Malchus, who lived in the second century B.C. Coins give further witness to the reign of Malchus III and his queen Shaquilath.

Rabilus (Rabbel) II is the last-known Nabataean king. His reign began about A.D. 70/71, and apparently he was the Nabataean ruler at the time of Trajan's annexation of Arabia. Riddle points out that he assumed the crown as a minor under the regency of his mother.[8] Though the historians have very little to say about his accomplishments, a large number of inscriptions have been found that speak of some of his activities as well as of the Nabataean kingdom over which he ruled. An inscription dating early in his reign probably speaks of some kind of disaster from which Rabilus saved his people. What the danger was is not known—perhaps it was of a military nature. In translation, it reads:

> This is the cella (?) which was made Murlim and Adi and Hur over the al[tar of the god.............in the year] two of Rabb [el, the king of the Nabataeans who roused and delivered his people].[9]

Another inscription, of a similar nature, dates to the twenty-third year of his reign. It reads:

> This is the chippus offered by Mumath, son of Gadipu, to Dushara and A ra the god of our lord who is in Bosra,

---

6. Enno Littman, "Nabataean Inscriptions" in *Semitic Inscriptions,* Publications of the Princeton University Archaeological Expedition to Syria in 1904-1905, 4th div., sect. A (Leyden: E. J. Brill Publishers and Printers, 1914), pp. 21-22.
7. Johnny Marion Riddle, "Political History of the Nabataeans from the Time of Roman Intervention until Loss of Independence in 106 A.D." (M.A. thesis, University of North Carolina, 1961), p. 130.
8. Ibid.
9. Littman, "Nabataean Inscriptions," pp. 2-3.

in the 23rd year of King Rabel, king of the Nabataeans,
who brought life and deliverance to his people.[10]

What the circumstances were that led to these inscriptions still
remains a mystery. It is possible that they were military engage-
ments, although history records no such events in which Rabilus
and the Nabataeans were involved. Another possibility is that this
is a title which he constantly used, just as Aretas IV was known
as "the lover of his people."

Under Rabilus, the Nabataeans maintained their distinct identity as agriculturists, as is indicated by Negev's statement:

> A considerable number of Nabataean inscriptions dated to
> the years 18 and 28 of his [Rabbel] reign, A.D. 88 and 98,
> have been discovered at Oboda and in its agricultural hinter-
> land. They bear witness to that period's extensive activities,
> especially in the construction of agricultural installations.[11]

Extant coins from the period of his reign indicate that he was
married to Gamilath who was also his queen.[12] The obverse of
his coins shows a bust of the king with the inscription, "Rabbel the
king, king of Nabataea." The reverse shows a bust of Gamilath
with the inscription "Gamilath, his sister, queen of Nabataea."[13]

When Rabilus came to the throne, Vespasian had been ruling
in Rome for just a short time. During his reign as king of the
Nabataeans, Rabilus saw five different emperors sit upon the
throne in Rome.[14] His was a period of peace; there are no
records of any major military activities in which the Nabataeans
were involved, unless the two inscriptions cited above are so interpreted. There were no hostilities between the Judaeans and the

---

10. George Allen Cooke, *A Textbook of North-Semitic Inscriptions:
Phoenician, Aramaic, Nabataean, Palmyrene, Jewish* (Oxford: At the
Clarendon Press, 1903), pp. 254-255.
11. A. Negev, "Oboda, Mampsis, and Provincia Arabia," *Israel Exploration Journal* 27, no. 1 (1967): 47.
12. George Francis Hill, "The Ancient Coinage of Southern Arabia" in
Proceedings of the British Academy (London: Humphrey Milford,
1915-1916), p. 12.
13. Ibid.
14. Vespasian, A.D. 69-79; Titus, A.D. 79-81; Domitian, A.D. 81-96;
Nerva, A.D. 96-98; Trajan, A.D. 98-117.

Nabataeans during his reign because Jerusalem had been destroyed and the Romans had taken over Judaea just prior to his coming to the throne.

In A.D. 106, Nabataean independence came to an end. Trajan was the Roman ruler under whom this came about. Rome official-ly annexed into the Roman Empire all of Arabia, and it became known as *Provincia Arabia*. There is much discussion about the circumstances surrounding this event. Was there some particular event or series of events that brought about Rome's action? There might have been a few minor border incidents, but there had been no major clashes. Riddle says, ". . . there were sufficient grounds for the decision in the need of a provincial control of Arabia to protect the potentially rich, and, more important, to tap effectively the trade route between the Red Sea and Syria."[15] Had the Naba-taean power crumbled, and the Romans saw this as their oppor-tunity to accomplish a takeover? Crystal Bennett makes this implication when she says, "It was only when the royal power weakened under their last ruler, Rabbel [Rabilus] II, and when the Roman Empire was controlled by one of its greatest empire-builders, the emperor Trajan, that this proud kingdom lost its independence."[16]

This need not be the case, however. It is not unreasonable to believe that the Nabataeans offered little if any opposition. Trajan himself did not even come to Arabia; rather he sent Palma, the governor of Syria, to effect the change. Dio Cassius simply says: "About this time, Palma, the governor of Syria, subdued the part of Arabia around Petra and made it subject to the Romans."[17] The following statement of Negev indicates that there was no hostility involved and that the Nabataean culture continued after the Ro-man annexation:

> Two additional inscriptions belonging to the years 2 and 20 of the Province speak explicitly of "building" and "mak-ing." These inscriptions are of utmost importance, as they

15. Riddle, "Political History of the Nabataeans," p. 134.
16. Crystal M. Bennett, "The Nabataeans in Petra," *Archaeology* 15, no. 4 (Winter 1962): 234.
17. Dio Cassius, *Dio's Roman History,* trans. Earnest Cary, The Loeb Classical Library, vol. 6 (New York: G. P. Putnam's Sons, n.d.), p. 21.

Architrave from Khirbet et-Tannur. *ASOR*

Nabataean architectural remains with a floral pattern from Khirbet Brak near Petra. *ASOR*

prove the continuation of these activities from the late Nabataean period into the years following the establishment of the *Provincia Arabia*. They also add weight to the opinion of those who maintain that the annexation of the Nabataean realm did not involve hostilities.[18]

While commenting on the results of archaeological work done at Oboda, Negev stated that the city was

> . . . reoccupied by the Nabataeans during the second half of King Rabel [Rabbel, Rabilus] II's reign, from about A.D. 88. The many building activities, especially those of agricultural installations, continued as late as A.D. 126, well after the dissolving of the Nabataean kingdom and its transformation into the *Provincia Arabia*.[19]

Outside of the governmental change that took place, the only other major change was that the capital was moved from Petra to Bosra in the north. The annexation dealt a death blow to the trade of Petra, and Bosra became not only the political center of the new province but also the commercial center. This explains why in Roman times the city of Petra was greatly reduced in size in comparison to what it had been under the Nabataeans.

The annexation of Nabataea into the Roman Empire in A.D. 106 thus brought to an official end the long period of Nabataean independence and prominence. This political maneuver eventually led to the end of the Nabataean culture and civilization, but it by no means ended its influence. The legacy of the Nabataeans lives on in that land today.

---

18. Negev, "Oboda, Mampsis, and Provincia Arabia," p. 47.
19. A. Negev, "The Date of the Petra-Gaza Road," *Palestine Exploration Quarterly,* January-June 1966, p. 95.

Appendix A

Petra

Among all the ancient cities of the Near and Middle East, Petra stands unique. To this very day its massive tombs and temples serve as proof of its durability. Much of it was not built; it was hewn. This is one of the two reasons why so much of it still stands today. The other reason is attributed to the fact that it was almost impregnable as long as there were able-bodied men within its confines who could defend it. The enemy, therefore, was unable to enter the city and carry out full-scale destruction, as was done at so many occupied sites throughout Palestine. The Nabataeans were mainly responsible for the massive architecture that visitors to the city see yet today.

The words of Dean Burgon's prize sonnet, "Petra," speak of the splendor of that great city:

> It seems no work of man's creative hand
> by labor wrought as wavering fancy planned:
> But from the rock as if by magic grown,
> Eternal, silent, beautiful, alone!
> Not virgin white, like that old Doric shrine
> where erst Athens held her rites divine;
> Not saintly-grey, like many a minster fane
> That crowns the hill and consecrates the plane;
> But rosy-red, as if the blush of dawn
> That first beheld them were not yet withdrawn;
> The dues of youth upon a brow of woe,
> Which man deemed old two thousand years ago.
> Match me such marvel save in Eastern clime.
> A rose-red city, held as old as time.

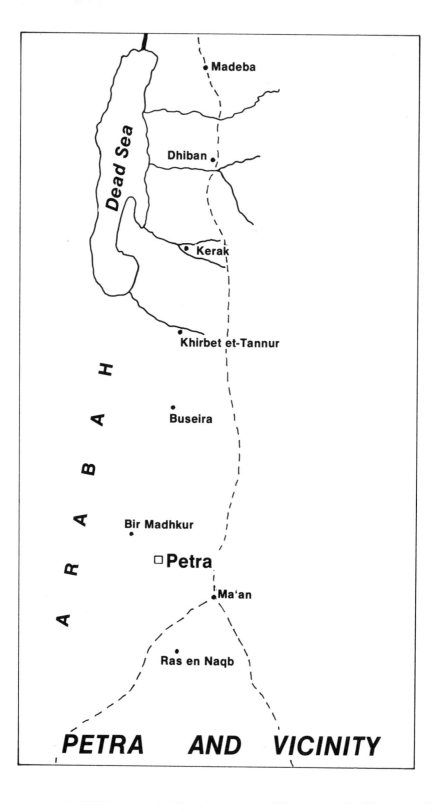

PETRA AND VICINITY

Nabataean tombs at Petra, in which the striation of the rock is clearly visible. *John I. Lawlor*

These words probably are more meaningful to those who have had the good fortune of visiting the city.[1] It is an experience in "true technicolor." It is impossible to imagine the color of the city; even colored slides or photographs cannot fully convey what is to be seen by the human eye. Crystal Bennett very eloquently describes colorful Petra:

> The multi-colored striations of blue, white, yellow and black give the sandy rocks a scenic brilliance and magnificence. The colors change with the play of light so that Petra never presents the same aspect for more than a few minutes. This ever-changing color presents a challenge to the photographic skill of visitors, whose number daily increases.[2]

1. On two successive days (April 18-19, 1967), this writer had the extreme good fortune of visiting Petra. This was made possible through the generosity of Mrs. Eleanor K. Vogel of Cincinnati, Ohio; and for this outstanding experience, this writer is deeply indebted to her.
2. Crystal M. Bennett, "The Nabataeans in Petra," *Archaeology* 15, no. 4 (Winter 1962):234.

It already has been pointed out that Petra has had a long history and that it was inhabited long before the Nabataeans made their entrance onto the scene. As early as 1905, Libbey and Hoskins, after making an extensive trip through this region, stated that the "Horites, Edomites, Nabataeans, and Romans . . . all rejoiced and boasted in the possession of this unique stronghold."[3] It is very important to remember, however, that this statement was made not on the basis of excavation, but rather on the basis of surface sherding at best. Since that time, excavators have worked at Petra; and their work has confirmed earlier occupation. Libbey and Hoskins's reference to Horite possession of the city must be called into question on the basis of the lack of evidence. Probably this theory was based upon the old and faulty etymology that understood Horites as "cave-dwellers."

3. William Libbey and Franklin E. Hoskins, *The Jordan Valley and Petra* (New York: G. P. Putnam's Sons, 1905), p. 64.

Nabataean cave dwellings at Petra. *John I. Lawlor*

The mountains of Petra. *John I. Lawlor*

The entrance into the narrow pass leading into Petra. Note the water channel at the left. *John I. Lawlor*

Looking at Petra from the southeast, the mountains hide any evidence of a city. As one walks through the narrow ravine, the sheer cliffs begin to rise high overhead; and he gets the feeling of insignificance. During the days of the Nabataeans, a huge channel was cut in the wall of rock—this carried water into the city of Petra and to its inhabitants. This channel is now choked with fallen rock and other debris. In places the cliffs above almost touch; the effect is that one is in "perpetual twilight" as he makes the lonely but fascinating trek through the Siq. It is natural to wonder, while walking through it, how this phenomenon came to be. Various theories have been propounded in an attempt to answer this question. Two of the most popular theories are: first, that through a countless number of years a stream relentlessly rushed over this path leaving its mark forever embedded in the rock; and second, that a great geological upheaval resulted in the splitting of these massive mountains of rock. After walking for half to three-quarters of an hour,[4] one suddenly sees a break in the great chasm a few feet ahead. This scene has given rise to the familiar photograph of half of the Khazneh framed by the cliffs of the Siq.[5] At this point, the visitor is first introduced to the glory and splendor of this great rock city. It is most appropriately named "Petra," for *petra* (πέτρα) is the Greek word for "rock."

Miss Bennett gives a brief history of the archaeological work that has been carried out at Petra:

> Archaeological excavation began in the early 1930's, but the main interest at that time was not primarily the city area. In addition, excavation techniques were not yet sufficiently advanced to enable the establishment of a detailed stratigraphic picture of the city's history. From 1954 to 1956 the Department of Antiquities of Jordan sponsored a program of clearance and preservation in the heart of the

---

4. George Livingston Robinson states that the Siq is one and one-fourth miles long. G. L. Robinson, ed., *The Sarcophagus of an Ancient Civilization: Petra, Edom and the Edomites* (New York: The Macmillan Co., 1930), p. 12.

5. See the cover photograph of *Natural History* 73, no. 2 (February 1964).

Niche carved into the wall at the entrance of the siq where Nabataean deity "stood guard." *John I. Lawlor*

The narrow ravine leading into Petra. *John I. Lawlor*

city. A long stretch of the main Roman street, with remains of buildings on either side, was uncovered, but analysis of the stratigraphy was outside the scope of the work. A detailed knowledge of Petra's history and of the development of Nabataean material culture was still lacking.

The chief aim of the recent excavations has been to fill this gap. In particular, stratified evidence has been sought of the city's history while it was still the capital of the independent Nabataean kingdom. Excavations were inaugurated in 1958 by the British School of Archaeology in Jerusalem, under the direction of Peter J. Parr. For part of the 1959 season the work was carried on jointly by the British School and an American group; Dr. Philip Hammond (then of Lycoming College) was Assistant Director. In 1959 and 1960 the Department of Antiquities of Jordan also cooperated, owing to the active interest of its Director, Dr. Awni Dajani.[6]

In addition, rather extensive work has been done on the Con-

---

6. Bennett, "The Nabataeans in Petra," p. 237.

way High Place[7] as well as on Umm el-Biyara.[8] In regard to the latter, there is a discussion between scholars over the identification of Umm el-Biyara with the Sela of II Kings 14:7. There is one school of thought that believes that such an identification is to be made;[9] there is another which says that such an identification cannot be legitimately made.[10] The excavator of Umm el-Biyara draws this conclusion:

7. Ray L. Cleveland, "The Excavation of the Conway High Place [Petra] and Soundings at Khirbet Ader," *The Annual of the American Schools of Oriental Research*, vol. 34, 35 (1960).
8. Crystal M. Bennett, "Exploring Umm el-Biyara, the Edomite Fortress-rock Which Dominates Petra," *The London Illustrated News*, April 30, 1966.
9. Denis Baly, *The Geography of the Bible*, (New York: Harper and Row, Publishers, 1957), p. 245. Nelson Glueck, "Explorations in Eastern Palestine II," *Annual of the American Schools of Oriental Research* 15 (1934-35).
10. Jean Starcky, "Petra et al Nabatene," *Supplement au Dictionnaire De La Bible*, trans. unknown, (1964).

The great high place at Petra. *ASOR*

It is true that the main purpose of the excavation, to prove
that Umm el-Biyara was Biblical Sela, has not been achieved.
All that can be said in this connection is that the evidence of
pottery and small finds points to the earliest occupation years
later, mainly in the seventh century B.C.[11]

Some notable discoveries that shed some light on the Nabataean
culture in Petra have been made through the excavator's spade. In
the southern part of the city, excavations uncovered a well-con-
structed Nabataean house. The walls of this house, parts of which
are still standing, reached a height of three meters. It was a rather
imposing building; there was a large rectangular-shaped courtyard
in the center, with several rooms opening off this courtyard on
both sides. Only two other buildings of Nabataean origin and in
such good repair have been found: one at Dhiban; the other at
Abda (Avdat).[12] A second factor worthy of mention is the evidence of town planning.[13] These discoveries demonstrate the settled
character of the Nabataean culture achieved in Petra. They also
present clear evidence of the "building know-how" that they
possessed.

Most impressive to the visitors of Petra are the rockhewn
tombs and temples. Many of these seem to bear the influence of
Hellenism. If this be true, it undoubtedly came from Egypt, where
Alexander had made definite Hellenistic inroads. However, it is
difficult to determine just when some of them came into existence.
Robinson makes this same point:

> Was it originally a temple or tomb, monument or gather-
> ing place? And did the many cuttings, winding steps, cham-
> bers, ruined building, sacrificial places and tombs, belong
> to the period of its construction, or might not some of
> them have been far earlier? We could but guess; we let
> our imaginations run riot, but none of us know, nor is it
> easy to know.[14]

---

11. Bennett, "The Nabataeans in Petra," p. 31.
12. A detailed description of this house is included in C. M. Bennett's
"The Nabataeans in Petra," *Archaeology* 15, no. 4 (Winter 1962):
238-240.
13. Ibid., p. 238.
14. G. L. Robinson ed., *The Sarcophagus of an Ancient Civilization*,
p. 76.

The great Urn Tomb at Petra. Carved in solid rock, 5th century B.C. *John I. Lawlor*

The combination of the colors of the rock and the massive architecture make these structures most remarkable. They stand today as a constant testimony to the engineering ability of their originators.

This was the capital of the Nabataean Empire. Its location was strategic, for it was right in line with major trade routes going north-south and east-west. This made it a pivotal point for the caravans going in all directions. For this reason, it became a very wealthy city. In A.D. 106, the Romans, under Trajan, absorbed the Nabataean Empire into the Roman Empire, making their territory into the province of Arabia. This was not, however, the end of Petra's history. This great city lived on. The size of Petra, however, was reduced after the Romans took control of it.

One last matter in relation to Petra is of an eschatological nature. There is a popular school of thought that believes that Petra is the place to which the Jews will flee during the period of the Great Tribulation after the antichrist breaks his treaty with them. This theory got its start sometime toward the end of

Nabataean monuments at Petra. *John I. Lawlor*

Nabataean monuments at Petra. *John I. Lawlor*

the nineteenth century and the beginning of the twentieth. It was particularly popular then. This was based upon such Scripture passages as Matthew 24:15-26; Mark 13:14-23; Isaiah 2:17-22 and others. In addition to this, the fact that half a century ago Petra was difficult to reach by land made this theory quite attractive to some. Inside Petra, the mountains are dotted with caves; and, of course, the location could easily have been defended against a mass army of foot soldiers. All of these factors put together seemed to lend support to this view.

Several of these factors have changed in more recent years, however, and these changes render this theory implausible. In the first place, Petra is no longer hard to reach by land. Paved roads now take the traveler practically right up to the doorstep of the Siq. Another fact is that the city is no longer so easily defended against all the mechanization of modern warfare. King Hussein of Jordan demonstrated this by landing a helicopter in the basin of the city. With the possibility of invading this location by air, it, in turn, could easily become a trap for those who might seek refuge inside. These factors alone make such a theory untenable.

Appendix B

Aelius Gallus's Expedition into Arabia According to Strabo*

Many of the special characteristics of Arabia have been disclosed by the recent expedition of the Romans against the Arabians, which was made in my own time under Aelius Gallus as commander. He was sent by Augustus Caesar to explore the tribes and the places, not only in Arabia, but also in Aethiopia, since Caesar saw that the Troglodyte country which adjoins tribes and the places, not only in Arabia, but also in Aethiopia, which separates the Arabians from the Troglodytes, is extremely narrow. Accordingly he conceived the purpose of winning the Arabians over to himself or of subjugating them. Another consideration was the report, which had prevailed from all time, that they were very wealthy, and that they sold aromatics and the most valuable stones for gold and silver, but never expended with outsiders any part of what they received in exchange; for he expected either to deal with wealthy friends or to master wealthy enemies. He was encouraged also by the expectation of assistance from the Nabataeans, since they were friendly and promised to co-operate with him in every way.

Upon these considerations, therefore, Gallus set out on the

*Strabo, *The Geography of Strabo,* trans. Horace Leonard Jones, The Loeb Classical Library, 8 vols. (Cambridge: Harvard University Press, 1961), 7:353-363.

expedition; but he was deceived by the Nabataean Administrator, Syllaeus, who, although he had promised to be guide on the march and to supply all needs and to co-operate with him, acted treacherously in all things, and pointed out neither a safe voyage along the coast nor a safe journey by land, misguiding him through places that had no roads and by circuitous routes and through regions destitute of everything, or along rocky shores that had no harbours or through waters that were shallow or full of submarine rocks; and particularly in places of that kind, flood-tides, as also the ebb-tides, caused very great distress. Now this was the first mistake of Gallus, to build long boats, since there was no naval war at hand, or even be expected; for the Arabians are not very good warriors even on land, rather being hucksters and merchants, to say nothing of fighting at sea. But Gallus built not less than eight boats . . . at Cleopatris, which is near the old canal which extends from the Nile. But when he realized that he had been thoroughly deceived, he built one hundred thirty vessels of burden, on which he set sail with about ten thousand infantry, consisting of Romans in Aegypt, as also of Roman allies, among whom were five hundred Jews and one thousand Nabataeans under Syllaeus. After many experiences and hardships he arrived in fourteen days at Leuce Come in the land of the Nabataeans, a large emporius, although he had lost many of his boats, some of these being lost, crews and all, on account of difficult sailing, but not on account of any enemy. This was caused by the treachery of Syllaeus, who said that there was no way for an army to go to Leuce Come by land; and yet camel traders travel back and forth from Petra to this place in safety and ease, and in such numbers of men and camels that they differ in no respect from any army.

This came to pass because Obodas, the king, did not care much about public affairs, and particularly military affairs (this is a trait common to all the Arabian kings), and because he put everything in the power of Syllaeus; and because Syllaeus treacherously out-generalled Gallus in every way, and sought, as I think, to spy out the country and, along with the Romans, to destroy some of its cities and tribes, and then to establish himself lord of all, after the Romans were wiped out by hunger and fatigue and diseases and any other evils which he had treacherously contrived for them. However, Gallus put in at Leuce Come, his army now being sorely tried both with scurvy and with lameness in the leg, which are native ailments. . . . At all events, he was forced to spend both the summer and the winter there, waiting for the sick to recover. Now the loads of aromatics are conveyed from Leuce Come to Petra, and thence to Rhinocolura, which is in Phoenicia near Aegypt, and thence to the other peoples; but at the present time they are for the most part transported by the Nile to Alexandria; and they are landed from Arabia and India at Myus Harbour; and then they are conveyed by camels over to Coptos in Thebais, which is situated on a canal of the Nile, and then to Alexandria. Again Gallus moved this army from Leuce Come and marched through regions of such kind that water had to be carried by camels, because of the baseness of the guides; and therefore it took many days to arrive at the land of Aretas, a kinsman of Obodas. Now Aretas received him in a friendly way and offered him gifts, but the treason of Syllaeus made difficult the journey through that country too; at any rate, it took thirty days to traverse the country, which afforded only zeia,[1] a few palm trees, and butter instead of oil, because they passed through parts that had no roads.

But the man who was responsible for this failure, I mean Syllaeus, paid the penalty at Rome, since, although he pretended friendship, he was convicted, in addition to his rascality in this matter, of other offences too, and was beheaded.

---

1. A kind of coarse grain.

Appendix C

A Comparison of Nabataean King Lists

C.I.S.[1]	LITTMAN[2]	STARCKY[3]	RIDDLE[4]	LAWLOR[5]
Aretas I	*Aretas I*	*Aretas I*	*Aretas I*	*Aretas I*
Malchus I			*Malchus I*	*Malchus I*
Erotimus			*Erotimus*	*Erotimus*
Aretas II	*Aretas II-Erotimus*	*Aretas II*	*Aretas II*	*Aretas II*
Obodas I	*Obodas I*	*Obodas I*	*Rabilus I*	*Obodas I*
Rabilus I	*Rabb'el I*	*Rabbel I*	*Obodas I*	*Rabilus I*
Aretas III	*Aretas III*	*Aretas III*	*Aretas III*	*Aretas III*
	Obodas II			
Malchus II	*Malchus I*	*Malchus I*	*Malchus II*	*Malchus II*
Obodas II	*Obodas III*	*Obodas II*	*Obodas II*	*Obodas II*
Aretas IV	*Aretas IV*	*Aretas IV*	*Aretas IV*	*Aretas IV*
Malchus III	*Malchus II*	*Malchus II*	*Malchus III*	*Malchus III*
Rabilus II	*Rabb'el II*	*Rabbel II*	*Rabilus II*	*Rabilus II*
	Malchus III			

1. *Corpus Inscriptionum Semiticarum,* (Paris, 1902), pp 181-182.
2. Enno Littman, "Nabataean Inscriptions" in *Semitic Inscriptions,* Publications of the Princeton University Archaeological Expedition to Syria in 1904-1905, 4th div., sect. A (Leyden: E. J. Brill Publishers and Printers, 1914), p. viii.
3. Jean Starcky, "The Nabataeans: A Historical Sketch," *The Biblical Archaeologist* 18, no. 4 (December 1955): 88-101.
4. Johnny Marion Riddle, "Political History of the Nabataeans from the Time of Roman Intervention until Loss of Independence in 106 A.D." (M.A. thesis, University of North Carolina, 1961).
5. This king list has been drawn up on the basis of a comparison of the other king lists, together with a consultation of various histories.

Bibliography

Literary

The Apocrypha According to the Authorized Version. Oxford: The University Press, n.d.

Appian. *Appian's Roman History.* Translation by Horace White. 4 vols. The Loeb Classical Library. New York: The Macmillan Co., 1912.

Bible:
The King James Version
New American Standard Bible—New Testament
The American Standard Version
The Greek New Testament. Edited by Kurt Aland, Matthew Black, Bruce Metzger, and Allen Wikgren. Stuttgart, West Germany: Wurttemburg Bible Society, 1966.

Dio Cassius. *Dio's Roman History.* Translation by Earnest Cary. 9 vols. The Loeb Classical Library. New York: G. P. Putnam's Sons.
————. *Dio's Rome.* Translation by H. B. Foster. Troy, New York: Pafraets Book Company, 1905.

Diodorus. *Diodorus of Sicily.* Translation by C. H. Oldfather, C. L. Sherman, C. Bradford Wells, Russel M. Geer, and F. R. Walton. 10 vols. Loeb Classical Library. New York: G. P. Putnam's Sons, 1933.

Godolphin, Francis R. B., ed. *The Greek Historians.* 2 vols. "Herodotus," vol. 1, translated by George Rawlinson. New York: Random House Publishers, 1942.

Josephus, Flavius. *The Life and Works of Flavius Josephus.* Translated by William Whiston 1867. Reprint. Grand Rapids: Kregel Publications, 1964.

Pliny. *The History of the World.* Translation by Philemon Holland. London: Centaur Press Ltd., 1962.

Plutarch. *Plutarch's Lives.* The Translation called Dryden's. Corrected from the Greek and revised by A. H. Glough. 5 vols. New York: Bigelow, Brown & Co., n.d.

Strabo. *The Geography of Strabo.* Translation by Horace Leonard Jones. 8 vols. The Loeb Classical Library. Cambridge, Mass.: Harvard University Press, 1961.

Tacitus, Cornelius. *The Works of Cornelius Tacitus with an Essay on His Life and Genius.* Translation by Arthur Murphy. Philadelphia: Thomas Wardle, 1844.

Archaeological

Aharoni, Y.; Evenari, M.; Shanan, L.; Tadmor, N. H. "The Ancient Desert Agriculture of the Negev" (Part V. An Israelite Agricultural Settlement at Ramat Matred). *Israel Exploration Journal* 10 (1960).

Amiran, Ruth. *Ancient Pottery of Erez-Yisra'el.* Jerusalem: Department of Antiquities, 1958.

Bennett, Crystal M. "Exploring Umm el Biyara, the Edomite Fortress-rock Which Dominates Petra." *The London Illustrated News,* 30 April 1966.

————. "The Nabataeans in Petra." *Archaeology* 15 (Winter 1962).

Cleveland, Ray L. "The Excavation of the Conway High Place (Petra) and Soundings at Khirbet Ader." *The Annual of the American Schools of Oriental Research* 34-35 (1960).

Cooke, George Allen. *A Textbook of North-Semitic Inscriptions: Moabite, Hebrew, Phoenician, Aramaic, Nabataean, Palmyrene, Jewish.* Oxford: At the Clarendon Press, 1903.

Evenari, Michael and Koller, Dov. "Ancient Masters of the Desert." *Scientific American* 194 (April 1956).

Glueck, Nelson. "Explorations in Eastern Palestine II." *Annual of the American Schools of Oriental Research* 15 (1934-35).

————. "Explorations in Western Palestine." *Bulletin of the American Schools of Oriental Research,* no. 131 (October 1953).

————. "Exploring Southern Palestine (The Negev)." In *The Biblical Archaeologist Reader,* edited by George Ernest Wright and David Noel Freedman. Garden City, New York: Anchor Books, Doubleday and Company, Inc., 1961.

————. "Nabataean Torques," *The Biblical Archaeologist* 15, (May 1962).

————. "The Third Season of Explorations in the Negev," *Bulletin of the American Schools of Oriental Research,* no. 138 (April 1955).

Hammond, Philip C. "Desert Waterworks of the Ancient Nabataeans," *Natural History* 76 (June-July 1967).

————. "The Nabataean Bitumen Industry at the Dead Sea," *The Biblical Archaeologist* 23 (May 1959).

————. "Pattern Families in Nabataean Painted Ware," *American Journal of Archaeology* 63 (October 1959).

————. "Rose-Red City of Petra," *Natural History* 73 (February 1964).

Hill, George Francis. "The Ancient Coinage of Southern Arabia," *Proceedings of the British Academy*. London: Humphrey Milford, 1915-16.

————. *Catalogue of the Greek Coins of Arabia, Mesopotamia and Persia*. London: Longmans & Co., 1922.

Littmann, Enno. "Nabataean Inscriptions." In *Semitic Inscriptions*. Publications of the Princeton University of Archaeological Expedition to Syria in 1904-1905, 4th div., sect. A. Leyden: E. J. Brill Publishers and Printers, 1914.

————. "Nabataean Inscriptions from Egypt I," *Bulletin of the School of Oriental and African Studies* 15 (1953).

————. "Nabataean Inscriptions from Egypt II." *Bulletin of the School of Oriental and African Studies* 16 (1954).

Luckenbill, David Daniel. *Ancient Records of Assyria and Babylonia.* 2 vols. Chicago: University of Chicago Press, 1926.

Negev, A. "The Date of the Petra-Gaza Road." *Palestine Exploration Quarterly* (January-June 1966).

————. "New Dated Nabataean Graffiti from the Sinai." *Israel Exploration Journal* 17 (1967).

————. "Nabataean Inscriptions from 'Avdat (Oboda)." *Israel Exploration Journal* 16 (1961).

————. "Nabataean Inscriptions from 'Avdat (Oboda)." *Israel Exploration Journal* 13 (1963).

————. "Oboda, Mampsis, and Provincia Arabia." *Israel Exploration Journal* 17 (1967).

————. "Stonedresser's Marks from a Nabataean Sanctuary at 'Avdat." *Israel Exploration Journal* 15 (1965).

Pritchard, James B. *Ancient Near Eastern Texts*. Princeton University Press, 1955.

Rabinowitz, Isaac. "Aramaic Inscriptions of the Fifth Century B.C.E. from a North-Arab Shrine in Egypt." *Journal of Near Eastern Studies* 15 (January 1956).

Shanan, L.; Evenari, M.; Tadmor, N. H. "Rainfall Patterns in the Central Negev Desert." *Israel Exploration Journal* 17 (1967).

Starkey, J. and Strugnell, J. "Deux nonvelles inscriptions nabat'enes (Plauches 8-9)." *Revue Biblique,* no 2, April 1966.

Tushingham, A. D. "The Excavations at Dibon (Dhîbân) in Moab." *The Annual of the American Schools of Oriental Research* 40 (1972).

Winnet, Fred V. and Reed, William L. "The Excavations at Dibon (Dhîbân) in Moab." *The Annual of the American Schools of Oriental Research* 36-37 (1964).

BIBLIOGRAHY

SECONDARY SOURCES

Historical

Albright, William F. *History, Archaeology, and Christian Humanism.* New York: McGraw-Hill Book Co., 1969.

Baly, Denis. *The Geography of the Bible.* New York: Harper and Row, Publishers, 1957.

Barger, Thomas C. "Notes on the Nabataeans." *Aramco World* (special issue) "Arabia the Beautiful," 16 (September-October 1965).

Bevan, Edwyn, *Jerusalem Under the High Priests.* London: Edward Arnold Publishers, 1958.

Chapot, Vincent. *The Roman World.* New York: Alfred A. Knopf, 1928.

Cook, S. A.; Adcock, F. E.; Charlesworth, M. P., eds. *The Cambridge Ancient History,* 12 vol. Cambrige, England: At the University Press, 1930.

Crevier, John Baptist Lewis. *The History of the Roman Emperors from Augustus to Constantine.* Translation by John Mill, Esq. 10 vols. London: C. & J. Rivington, 1814.

Eckenstein, Lina. *A History of Sinai.* New York: The Macmillan Co., 1921.

Eddy, Samuel K. *The King Is Dead.* Lincoln: University of Nebraska Press, 1961.

Fairweather, William. *The Background of the Gospels.* Edinburgh, Scotland: T. & T. Clark, 1926.

————. *From the Exile to the Advent.* Edinburgh: T. & T. Clark, 1947.

Falconer, William. "Preface." In *Strabo's Geography.* 3 vols. London: Henry G. Bohn, 1858.

Faris, Nabih Amin, ed. *The Arab Heritage.* New York: Russell and Russell, Inc., 1963.

Farmer, William Reuben. *Maccabees, Zealots, and Josephus.* New York: Columbia University Press, 1956.

Finegan, Jack, *Light from the Ancient Past.* Princeton: Princeton University Press, 1959.

Frank, Tenney, ed. *An Economic Survey of Ancient Rome.* 5 vols. Baltimore: The Johns Hopkins Press, 1938.

Glueck, Nelson. *Deities and Dolphins.* New York: Farrar, Straus, and Giroux, 1965.

————. "The Nabataean Temple of Khirbet Tannur, Transjordan." *Bulletin of the Cincinnati Art Museum* 12 (January 1941).

————. *The River Jordan.* Philadelphia: The Westminster Press, 1946.

————. *Rivers in the Desert.* New York: American Book—Stratford Press, Inc., 1959.

147

Hammond, Philip C. "Petra." *The Biblical Archaeologist* 23 (February, 1960).

Hourain, George F. "Did Roman Commercial Competition Ruin South Arabia?" *Journal of Near Eastern Studies* 11 (October 1952).

Ibach, Robert D. and Lawlor, John. "Palestinian Pottery Chronology." Research Paper in Biblical Archaeology. Winona Lake, Ind.; Grace Theological Seminary, 1967.

Jones, Arnold Hugh Martin. *The Herods of Judae.* Oxford: Clarendon Press, 1938.

Kennedy, A. B. W. *Petra: Its History and Monuments.* London: Country Life, 1925.

Libbey, William and Hoskins, Franklin E. *The Jordan Valley and Petra.* New York: G. P. Putnam's Sons, 1905.

Mommsen, Theodor. *The History of Rome.* Translation by William Purdie Jackson. 5 vols. New York: Charles Scribner's Sons, 1895.
———. *The Provinces of the Roman Empire from Caesar to Diocletian.* Translation by William P. Dickson. 2 vols. New York: Charles Scribner's Sons, 1899.

Morris, Ya'akov. *Masters of the Desert.* New York: Putnam's Sons, 1961.

Morton, William H. "Umm el Biyara." *The Biblical Archaeologist* 19 (May 1956).

Murray, Margaret Alice. *Petra, The Rock City of Edom.* London: Blackie and Son, Ltd., 1939.

Olmstead, A. T. *History of Palestine and Syria.* 1931. Reprint. Grand Rapids: Baker Book House, 1965.

Perowne, Stewart H. *The Later Herods.* New York: Abingdon Press, 1958.
———. *The Life and Times of Herod the Great.* New York: Abingdon Press, 1966.

Petrie, W. M. Flinders, *Researches in Sinai.* London: John Murray, 1906.

Pfeiffer, Charles F. and Vos, Howard F. *The Wycliffe Historical Geography of Bible Lands.* Chicago: Moody Press, 1967.

Rapp, Robert S. "Josephus and Contemporary Historians." Seminar paper for New Testament Backgrounds. Winona Lake, Ind.: Grace Theological Seminary, 1966.

Riddle, Johnny Marion. "Political History of the Nabataeans from the Time of Roman Intervention until Loss of Independence in 106 A.D." Master's thesis, University of North Carolina, 1961.

Ritter, Carl. *The Comparative Geography of Palestine and the Sinaitic Peninsula,* vol. 1. New York: D. Appleton and Co., 1866.

Robinson, George Livingston, ed. *The Sarcophagus of an Ancient Civilization: Petra, Edom and the Edomites.* New York: The Macmillan Co., 1930.

Rostovtzeff, M. *Caravan Cities*. Translation by D. & T. Talbot Rice. Oxford: At the Clarendon Press, 1932.

————. *The Social and Economic History of the Roman Empire*. 2 vols. Oxford: At the Clarendon Press, 1957.

Schürer, Emil. *A History of the Jewish People in the Times of Jesus*. New York: Schocken Books, 1961.

Smith, George Adam. *Jerusalem*. 2 vols. London: Hodder & Stoughton, 1907.

————. *Assyrian Discoveries*. New York: Scribner, Armstrong, and Co., 1876.

————. *The Historical Geography of the Holy Land*. London: Hodder & Stoughton, 1898.

Starcky, Jean. "The Nabataeans: A Historical Sketch." *The Biblical Archaeologist* 28 (December 1955).

————. "Petra et la Nabatene." *Supplement au Dictionnaire de la Bible*. Translator not known. Paris: Letonzey & Ane, 1964.

Wright, George Ernest. *The Pottery of Palestine*. Ph. D. dissertation, John Hopkins University. Reprint. Ann Arbor: Edwards Brothers, Inc., 1937.

Encyclopedias, Lexicons, Charts, Commentaries, Atlases, and Bible Dictionaries

Angus, S. "Nabataeans." *The International Standard Bible Encyclopedia*, edited by James Orr, vol. 4. Grand Rapids: William B. Eerdmans Publishing Co., 1943.

Arndt, W. F. and Gingrich, F. W. *A Greek-English Lexicon of the New Testament and Other Early Christian Literature*. Chicago: The University of Chicago Press, 1957.

Barton, George A. "Nabataeans." *The Jewish Encyclopedia*, vol. 9. Edited by Isidore Singer. New York: Funk and Wagnalls, 1905.

Bauer, Theo. *Akkadische Lesestucke: Zeichenliste und Kommentar*, vol. 2. Rome: Pontifical Biblical Institute, 1953.

Beckwith, C. A. "The Nabataeans." *The New Schaff-Herzog Encyclopedia of Religious Knowledge*, edited by Samuel Macauley Jackson, vol. 8. New York: Funk and Wagnalls, 1910.

Boyer, James L. "Chart of the Period Between the Testaments." Winona Lake, Ind.: Grace Theological Seminary, 1962.

————. "New Testament Chronological Chart," Winona Lake, Ind.: Grace Theological Seminary, 1962.

Brown, Francis; Driver, S. R.; Briggs, Charles A. *A Hebrew and English Lexicon of the Old Testament*. Oxford: The Clarendon Press, 1962.

Clarke, Adam. "Second Epistle to the Corinthians." *Clarke's Commentary*, vol. 6. New York: Abingdon-Cokesbury Press, n.d.

149

Cooke, G. A. "Nabataeans." *Encyclopedia of Religion and Ethics,* edited by James Hastings, vol. 9. New York: Charles Scribner's Sons, 1928.

Cornfeld, Gaalyahu, ed. "Nabataeans." *Pictorial Biblical Encyclopedia.* Tel Aviv: Hamikra Baolam Publishing House Ltd., 1964.

Glueck, Nelson. "Nabataeans." *Twentieth Century Encyclopedia of Religious Knowledge,* edited by Lefferts A. Loetscher, vol. 2. Grand Rapids: Baker Book House, 1955.

Grollenberg, L. H. *Atlas of the Bible.* Camden: Thomas Nelson and Sons, 1965.

Keil, C. F. and Delitzsch, F. *Isaiah.* 2 vols. Grand Rapids: William B. Eerdmans Publishing Co., n.d.

——. *The Pentateuch.* 3 vols. Grand Rapids: William B. Eerdmans Publishing Co., n.d.

Larue, Gerald A. "Petra." In *The Biblical World.* Edited by Charles F. Pfeiffer. Grand Rapids: Baker Book House, 1966.

Lenski, R. C. H. *The Interpretation of I and II Corinthians.* Minneapolis: Augsburg Publishing House, 1937.

Malik, Butrus Abd al. "Arabia." In *The Biblical World.* Edited by Charles F. Pfeiffer. Grand Rapids: Baker Book House, 1966.

Millard, A. R. "Nabataeans," *The New Bible Dictionary.* Edited by J. D. Douglas. Grand Rapids: William B. Eerdmans Publishing Co., 1964.

Morren, N. "Nebaioth-Nabataeans." *The Popular and Critical Bible Encyclopedia,* edited by Samuel Fallows, vol. 2. Chicago: The Howard-Severance Co., 1908.

Plumptre, E. H. "The Acts of the Apostles." *Ellicott's Commentary on the Whole Bible,* edited by Charles John Ellicott, vols. 7-8. Grand Rapids: Zondervan Publishing House, 1959.

——. "The Second Epistle to the Corinthians." *Ellicott's Commentary on the Whole Bible,* edited by Charles John Ellicott, vols. 7-8. Grand Rapids: Zondervan Publishing House, 1959.

Thompson, J. A. "Nabataeans." *The Biblical World.* Edited by Charles F. Pfeiffer. Grand Rapids: Baker Book House, 1966.

General Index

Abarta, 110
Abath, 109
'Abd 'obodat, 110
Abda. *See* Avdat
Abia, 119-120
Abiabene, 120
Actium, Battle of, 57, 59
Adi, 122
Aelius Gallus, 19-20, 94-96, 98, 106, 140-142
Aeneas. *See* Aretas IV
Africa, 59, 69
Agala, 44
Agatharchides, 19
Agriculture, 12, 81-85
Aitibel, 110
Aklabu, 121
Aldelze, 110
Alexander (son of Herod the Great), 107
Alexander the Great, 30-31, 136
Alexander Jannaeus, 39-40, 42-44
Alexandra (daughter of John Hyrcanus), 62-63
Alexandra (wife of Alexander Jannaeus), 42-43
Alexandria, 35, 121, 142
Ali, 109
Allat, 121
Antichrist, 137
Antigonus, 55

Antigonus (general of Alexander the Great) 31-33
Antiochus, 55
Antiochus Epiphanes, 38
Antiochus VI (Sidetes), 38
Antiochus XII, 40, 42
Antipas. *See* Herod Antipas
Antipater (son of Herod the Great), 107
Antipater II, 53
Antipater (son of Herod the Great), 107
Appollodotus, 39
Aqaba, 69
Ara, 122
Arabah, 75
Arabia, 10, 12, 19, 22, 48, 59, 68-69, 93-95, 97-98, 105-106, 122, 124, 137, 140, 142
Aramaic language, 22
Archaeological explorations, 14-16, 20-25
Archelaus. *See* Herod Archelaus
Architecture, 12-14, 22-23, 129, 137
Aretas I, 37-38, 143
Aretas II, 39, 143
Aretas III, 40, 42-48, 50-54, 115, 143
Aretas IV, 17-18, 42, 97, 99, 103-121, 123, 143
Aristobulus, 107, 112

Index of Authors

Index of Texts